WE ARE NOT BORN SUBMISSIVE

We Are Not Born Submissive

How Patriarchy Shapes Women's Lives

Manon Garcia

PRINCETON UNIVERSITY PRESS

PRINCETON AND OXFORD

Requests for permission to reproduce material from this work
should be sent to permissions@press.princeton.edu

Published by Princeton University Press
41 William Street, Princeton, New Jersey 08540
6 Oxford Street, Woodstock, Oxfordshire OX20 1TR

press.princeton.edu

Library of Congress Cataloging-in-Publication Data

Names: Garcia, Manon, 1985– author.
Title: We are not born submissive : how patriarchy shapes women's lives /
    Manon Garcia.
Other titles: On ne naît pas soumise, on le devient. English
Description: Princeton : Princeton University Press, [2021] | "Originally
    published as On ne nait pas soumise on le devient © Climats, department of
    Flammarion, 2018." | Includes bibliographical references and index.
Identifiers: LCCN 2020035185 (print) | LCCN 2020035186 (ebook) |
    ISBN 9780691201825 (hardcover) | ISBN 9780691212623 (ebook)
Subjects: LCSH: Women—Psychology. | Feminism. | Dominance (Psychology) |
    Submissiveness. | Sexual dominance and submission. | Man-woman relationships.
Classification: LCC HQ1208 .G2713 (print) | LCC HQ1208 (ebook) |
    DDC 155.3/33–dc23
LC record available at https://lccn.loc.gov/2020035185
LC ebook record available at https://lccn.loc.gov/2020035186

British Library Cataloging-in-Publication Data is available

Editorial: Matt Rohal
Production Editorial: Kathleen Cioffi
Jacket Design: Sara Pinsonault
Production: Erin Suydam
Publicity: Maria Whelan and Amy Stewart

Jacket image by urfinguss / iStock

To Esther, Eve, and Salomé

Feminist books are generally a prospective memory of a movement which constantly needs to be taken up again; those of Mary Wollstonecraft and Simone de Beauvoir are also excellent philosophy books and should be read as such. Because books by women are all sectioned off under a special heading (by women, about women, for women), half their potential readers are deprived of solid reading matter.

—MICHÈLE LE DŒUFF, *HIPPARCHIA'S CHOICE*

One of the most important questions confronting all feminist theorists is why women, who are, after all, a majority in most populations, so often seem to submit to or even collude with their own subordination. At its simplest, the question is: why are not all women feminists?

—ALISON JAGGAR, *FEMINIST POLITICS AND HUMAN NATURE*

CONTENTS

Even the most independent and feminist women can catch themselves enjoying the conquering way in which men look at them, desiring to be a submissive object in the arms of their partner, or preferring domestic work—the small pleasures of well-folded laundry, of a pretty-looking breakfast table—to supposedly more fulfilling activities. Are these desires and pleasures incompatible with their independence? Do they betray the centuries of feminism that precede them? Can one expect men to "make the first move" and demand sex equality? The ambiguities of these topics are blindingly obvious in everyday life or when one opens a "women's" magazine: at the same time women are called upon to be free, to have their own careers, and to refuse any degrading treatment from men, these magazines overflow with advice and norms on the best ways to be an attractive sexual object, an obliging wife, a perfect mother.

In the aftermath of the scandal involving film producer Harvey Weinstein that gave rise to the #MeToo movement,[1] these contradictions became tangible in the comments made about the actresses involved: Were they sheer victims? Didn't they transform themselves, sometimes with a visible pleasure, into magnificent objects of men's desire? Weren't they simply trying to "sleep their way to the top"? These questions demonstrate a blindness to the realities of male domination as well as the way in which taboos about female submission are oftentimes superimposed onto this blindness. And the media have often taken sides with those who thought "pigs" had been "ratted on" too fast and that women liked to be "bothered."[2]

This book aims to analyze these apparent contradictions with the help of philosophy—especially the philosophy of Simone de Beauvoir. It does not seek to offer ready-made answers or solutions but rather to show the complexity of the world and of lived experiences. What is at stake is not to determine once and for all whether women are victims or fighters, whether men are guilty or not, whether what matters is the individual or the social structure. On the contrary, to examine women's submission to men is to study the complex ways in which gender hierarchies in society shape women's experiences.

1

Submission

A PHILOSOPHICAL TABOO

From Penelope patiently weaving the shroud as she waits for the return of Ulysses in the *Odyssey* to Anastasia reveling in the commands of Christian Grey in *Fifty Shades of Grey*, from *The Sexual Life of Catherine M.*[1] to *Desperate Housewives*, from Annie Ernaux's *The Possession*[2] to the actresses claiming for men a "right to bother" women, literature, movies, TV shows, and the news all stage and aestheticize a female submission that is chosen, sometimes professed, and appears as a source of satisfaction and pleasure. However, philosophy and feminist thought say very little, if anything, about this female submission. From a feminist point of view, considering that women could, in one way or another, choose and savor this submission appears as right wing, antifeminist, or even misogynistic; this idea seems to belong to the exclusive domain of those who believe in a feminine nature that would destine all females to a definitive submission to men. From the point of view of philosophers, especially canonical political philosophers, submission is a moral vice that goes against human nature. To submit oneself to another is to renounce one's most precious natural right: freedom. It thus seems impossible to *think*[3] this phenomenon whose multiple manifestations we constantly encounter nonetheless.

Anyone who wants to study female submission is presented with a general philosophical problem: the analysis of the concept of submission repeatedly stumbles upon the commonly held idea that wanting anything other than one's freedom goes against human nature. For this reason, in the history of philosophy, submission is rarely discussed; and when it is, it is seen as either a moral vice or a pathology. Rousseau thus writes in *The Social Contract*: "To renounce one's freedom is to renounce one's quality as a man, the rights of humanity, even its duties. There is no possible compensation for someone who renounces everything. Such a renunciation is incompatible with man's nature, and to deprive his will of all freedom is to deprive his actions of all morality."[4] There is something so taboo in the idea that human beings could submit themselves without being forced to that in the history of Western philosophy only the French philosopher of the sixteenth century Étienne de La Boétie and the creator of psychoanalysis, Sigmund Freud, have truly taken seriously the enigma of submission, albeit on different levels. La Boétie, in *Discourse on Voluntary Servitude*, is the first to wonder what makes the masses decide to obey a tyrant who dominates them when this tyrant only has power because the masses submit to him. La Boétie proposes a series of explanations, but ultimately he does not manage to conceive of this submission as something other than a moral vice of the masses, a faulty oversight of their natural freedom. Freud, in three texts that constitute the foundation of the psychoanalytic conception of masochism,[5] addresses not the masses' submission to a tyrant but what he calls masochism, the phenomenon of drawing pleasure from one's own moral or psychological pain. He conceives of masochism as the opposite of sadism. Freud easily proposes a psychoanalytic explanation of sadism, but his theory struggles with what he calls "the enigma of masochism." He identifies it as a pathology but does not manage to fully explain it. In general, philosophy fails to take seriously the fact that some people might want to obey other people and take pleasure in doing so.

When focusing specifically on female submission, the problem becomes even more complex. Historically, women's submission, unlike men's, has not been thought of as being contrary to human nature. Quite the opposite, submission is prescribed as the normal, moral, and natural behavior of women.[6] This valorization of submission goes hand in hand with the idea of an essential and natural inferiority of women compared to men: it is because women are viewed as incapable of being free in the way that men are, or that such a freedom is seen as a potential danger, that their submission is good. To consider that women submit voluntarily is, in such a context, sexist. It presupposes a difference of nature between men and women, on the basis of which women would be inferior to men. This inferiority is seen as both a weakness and an immorality: on the one hand, women submit to men because they are naturally weaker than men. They are passive in this submission. On the other hand, their weakness makes them morally inferior: women are basking in a submission that perfectly fits their nature and that they sometimes choose, whereas for men, who are authentically free subjects, submission is a moral vice.

In sum, we are at an impasse. Either we talk about female submission in its complexity, without remaining silent on the appeal that submission can have, which ostensibly places us on the side of the sexist tradition that makes submission women's natural destiny. Or we posit that men and women are equal and, in that case, women's submission, like men's, is either a moral vice or a pathology and is not really within the scope of philosophical inquiry. In the case of the latter, the only possible explanation for the valorization of female submission in cultural works is to see it as a manifestation of male domination in these passive victims that women would be. Thus, either one takes the appeal of submission for women seriously and adopts the sexist position of an immutable female nature, or one refuses the idea of a natural inferiority of women and, in that case, submissive women who are satisfied with this submission appear as passive victims or submissive beings that are guilty of not cherishing their freedom.

But then how can we explain that some of these works are written by women? Should we conclude that Catherine Millet, Annie Ernaux, and E. L. James are mistaken to such an extent that the experiences they mention should not even be considered? Against such an alternative between a sexist naturalization and an erasure of submission, one must directly confront these questions: Do women somewhat participate in patriarchy? If so, can this participation be considered voluntary or is it merely the result of the omnipotence of patriarchy? And, in a more polemical way, is submission necessarily bad? Is there, minimally, a form of pleasure taken in submission?

Female Submission and Feminism

Far from being sexist, focusing on women's submission can be resolutely feminist. Feminism is a theoretical enterprise and a political program aimed at promoting a certain form of equality between men and women—what this equality means, exactly, is a topic of debate among feminists themselves. The feminist agenda has many components and, at the fore, at least two: to shine a light on women's oppression *as* women and to fight this oppression.

This first part leads feminism to offer a social critique, which aims at showing that gender inequalities have a systematic character and that they are widespread and ongoing in such a way that they constitute a structural system of patriarchal oppression. In this way, the feminist movement has historically strived to bring women's oppression—in the context of male domination—to light by identifying the injustices encountered by women, both on an individual and on a social level, as well as this oppression's structural and widespread character. This first, theoretical, part (shining a light on women's oppression) is a precondition of the second part (the fight against sexist oppression) because it allows us to understand how oppression works. For instance, it shows that men's domination over women functions in a way that silences women and that systematically devalues their experiences and work—especially care work.

This first part also makes it possible to identify the mechanisms of domination that feminists need to fight and, as such, contributes to the construction of the second part. For instance, since the silencing of women is identified as one of the mechanisms of male domination, one of the elements of the feminist struggle against patriarchal oppression is ensuring that women's voices are being heard and recognized as important, in opposition to the patriarchal system in which men speak *in place of* women. In this respect, studying women's submission is a feminist enterprise as it consists in listening to women's experiences and taking them seriously, and in not deciding in advance that they are victims, guilty, passive, or perverse.

Most feminists have, however, carefully avoided the topic of female submission.[7] This can undoubtedly be explained by concern about adding grist to the conservatives' mill; they would have seen in such a topic the proof that feminists themselves believe in the submissive, maternal nature of women. Chauvinists are swift to conclude that women are submissive because they "like it" and to deny the structural effects of male domination. Remarks about domestic violence, which imply that if battered women do not speak up or leave it is probably because what they are experiencing is simply not that bad, are a paradigmatic example of this phenomenon. Evading talk about submission allows feminists to sidestep the risk of blaming the victims. This precaution is problematic, however, because it masks an important part of male domination: the complicity it elicits. One can, and must, study female submission without presuming that there is something typically or naturally feminine in this submission.

A concern here could be that in saying women are submissive, we might be implying that all women are and that there is nothing to do about that. To understand the fundamental difference between a study of female submission and the hypothesis of the eternal feminine—which is the name given to the theory of a natural submissive nature of women—one can turn toward linguistics and philosophy of language.[8] Two types of statements must be distinguished: (1) those uttered by the upholders of an eternal nature of women, who say "women are submissive"; and (2) those who say "some/most/all women are submissive" or "some/most/all women choose submission." The kind of generalization displayed in the first case, that is, generalizations that omit quantifiers, are called "generics" by linguists. The problem of generics is that they can—and are often taken to—imply that there is some necessary connection between the first and the second parts of their statement. In our case, it would mean that women are submissive by virtue of being women, that they are naturally submissive. In the second case, no hypothesis is made regarding the nature of femininity, but some singular experiences or forms of life are being taken seriously in their more or less widespread character. In using the second kind of statements, one is not stating that such a submission is good, bad, desirable, or normal; it only says that some/many/all women live in a situation of submission. Whereas the first statement can be seen as normative or essentialist, the statements of the second type are purely descriptive. Studying female submission is a feminist enterprise because it consists in describing an experience lived by women without considering this experience as absolute, natural, and necessary in order to be a woman.

In sum, my enterprise here is a feminist one in part because it adopts the perspective of women themselves as a starting point of the analysis and thus takes women's voices and experiences into account in the analysis of male domination. In the aftermath of the #MeToo movement, the world is seemingly divided into two camps: people who believe society is structured by the domination men exert over women, and those who think this domination either does not exist or is not that significant. Feminist works show that this separation is problematic because it is grounded on the assumption that only men's perspectives and actions matter. Fundamentally, even though the aim is to describe and contest women's position in society, when one talks of "male domination," one perpetuates the custom, long highlighted by feminist epistemologists, of systematically seeing the world from the perspective of men, understood as neutral and objective.[9] It is *men* who dominate or don't dominate, who seduce, who propose, who orgasm, who cheat, and who rape. This is not to say that investigating male domination is bad because in focusing on men it reproduces the habit of focusing the perspective on men, but that it is a feminist task to look at the phenomenon of male domination from the perspective of women.

Submission from Women's Point of View

Challenging the presumed objectivity of the male perspective and its systematic adoption is necessary both on a political level and on an epistemological one—that is, on the level of the construction of knowledge. On a political level, it is impossible to promote any sort of equality between men and women if this equality is to be built from a male perspective, that is, a perspective that may not take women's experience into account or fully understand it. For instance, some feminist philosophers have shown that classical political philosophy rests upon a distinction between a public and political sphere, which is reserved for men and in which individuals are conceived as independent from each other, and a private sphere, centered around the family, to which women are confined and in which people are linked to each other by relationships of love and dependency.[10] But classical political philosophy—up until the end of the twentieth century, according to Okin—conceals this distinction, despite depending on it, and thus excludes women from the political realm by default. Challenging the neutralized male perspective allows us to reveal the way male domination structures itself and makes itself durable.

As mentioned above, in addition to this political dimension, there is an epistemological one: challenging the hegemony of the male perspective and studying the world from women's perspective opens up a more complete understanding of the world that we inhabit. Marxists were the first to defend the idea that knowledge is situated and that the social position of agents grants them a specific perspective on the world. The perspective of the dominants and the one of the dominated do not open up the same understanding of the world. Yet what happens when one studies male domination and the issue of sex equality? The perpetuation of inequalities between men and women in Western societies, in which women have, overall, the same legal rights as men seems incomprehensible. If women have the same rights as men, have access to education, to jobs, to political offices, and yet find themselves in an inferior position in these domains, isn't it simply that they are less good than men or that they would rather "stay at home"? The obvious response to the enigma of the endurance of male domination, when the adopted perspective is the male one, is that women are now agents like any others and that if they are in an inferior position it is probably because of an inferior or different nature. But what does one see when looking at male domination from women's perspective? That in the face of a patriarchal system, even if women are naturally equal to men and have the same rights, submitting to men may be a rational choice.

This is not to say that *all* women are submissive or that there would be some sort of specific essence that would destine them to submission. It is merely an observation: very often, looking at male domination from women's point of view—from what this domination does to them—is to see the complexity and the ambiguity of this submission. It also reveals what in it can be both appealing and pleasurable, as well as alienating. Studying women's submission from women's point of view is not to say that only women bear responsibility in the endurance of male domination. On the contrary, it demonstrates what male domination does to women, how it is lived by women, and how it shapes their choices and their desires in a way that classical philosophy, in its methodological sexism, cannot grasp.

A Matter of Perspective

To study submission, one must first be sure to know exactly what is at stake in it. To begin with, talking about "submission" rather than "domination" is to decide to shift the perspective on power. There are numerous studies on domination, especially in political philosophy. But very few studies consider submission from the perspective of the submissive person rather than the dominant one. It seems to be taken for granted that submission does not need to be studied as such and that, in studying domination, one therefore understands submission, as if looking at domination in a mirror would provide us with a good understanding of submission. Against this tradition, La Boétie's originality in the *Discourse on Voluntary Servitude* lies in his examination of power from the bottom up, from the perspective of the tyrant's subjects, to understand what exactly their submission to the tyrant is. For all of his originality, however, La Boétie only thinks about submission in terms of the relationship between subjects and the tyrant or king, something he calls voluntary servitude and that is in a strictly political realm. Women's submission happens in the context of interpersonal relationships, not between the people and the government. In that sense, it does not belong to the political realm in a strict sense although it is political, since it concerns power relations; therefore his analyses are not directly useful in analyzing women's submission.

Adopting this same bottom-up approach in an interpersonal context—instead of a purely political one—requires that we begin with a descriptive and conceptual understanding of submission. At first glance, the identification of submission is dependent on a form of othering: people have a tendency to think only people who are "other" are submissive. A paradigmatic example of submission in the public debate in France is the veiled Muslim woman who lives in a working-class neighborhood—it is against this very image that the name of the once popular NGO Ni Putes Ni Soumises (Neither Whores nor

Submissives) was created.[11] From the point of view of French republicanism,[12] the Muslim woman is the paradigmatic manifestation of the absolutely submissive Other with whom it is impossible to identify.[13] In reality, however, we can identify a resemblance between a series of mundane, everyday experiences, which indicate that submission is not the morally faulty attitude of "others," of those who do not desire freedom: whether it is preferring to be under a boss's authority at work rather than be self-employed, even though this entails obeying someone; doing more than is asked by one's boss despite the negative impact this can have (this covers all instances of zeal at work—e.g., staying longer than required at one's place of work, working on weekends when we are not obligated to, etc.); recognizing one's inferiority to someone else, which justifies obeying him or her; or wanting to serve someone else without expecting anything in return (the unequal distribution of domestic work, for example). In the case of women in particular, submission is often presented as the experience of several subsets of women: veiled women, stay-at-home moms, battered wives. In reality, many women—not only categorical subsets—experience these forms or other forms of submission by the very fact of being women. There is submission in "dieting" or starving oneself to fit into a size 0. There is submission in the behavior of wives of academics or writers who are participating in the research and are not credited as coauthors. There is submission in taking up the entire mental load of the family. There is submission in accepting that men don't do their fair share of domestic work or parenting. Contrary to our first intuition about submission, most women are submissive in certain respects, and what distinguishes women from each other is more the degree of their submission than the fact that some women are submissive and others are not. Since submission is not an exceptional but a shared and mundane experience, it is all the more necessary to understand exactly what it consists of and in what ways it differs from domination, with which it is almost always associated.

Which Women?

This book aspires to examine women's submission in the inter-personal relationships between men and women in Western societies. Such a restriction of the study can, at first glance, look heteronormative and hegemonic; I do not think that this is the case (and I hope it is not).

To begin with, there are good reasons to focus on hetero-sexual relationships when studying female submission. Female submission is an interesting locus of analysis because a struc-tural dimension and an individual dimension are combined in it. Women's submission to men is prescribed by patriarchy, that is, the organization of society in a way that grants power to men and systematically disadvantages women as women. This submission is a component of the set of norms and ideological tenets of patriarchy and as such it is structural. There is also an individual dimension as women have enough leeway legally and socially for their actions to reflect, at least partially, their choices (it is always a certain person, in a certain situation, that submits to a certain other person). In non-heterosexual relationships, one can reasonably imagine that the structural dimension of submission is of lesser importance than in rela-tionships between men and women: the few studies devoted to the repartition of domestic work in lesbian couples support this hypothesis; they show that the unequal, gendered division of labor that is displayed in heterosexual relationships is almost completely absent among lesbian couples.[14] Focusing on heterosexual relationships does not imply that we see these as the norm but rather that we see in them the ultimate locus of the oppression of women by men.

I am restraining my analysis to Western[15] societies for two reasons. First, the greater women's freedom of choice, the more problematic their submission appears. The moral issues this book is focusing on appear when submission is not the result of clear coercion but appears as a choice. In this respect, focusing the analysis on the societies in which women and men are at least formally equal—that is to say, they have the same legal rights, overall—allows me to examine submission in its most morally complex forms.

Second, as we said earlier, one of the obstacles to a thorough examination of submission is the tendency to identify submission in others and not in oneself. In that regard, accusations of submission have been part of an imperialist process of othering women from non-Western worlds. The philosopher Uma Narayan, who highlighted these processes of imperialist othering,[16] studied the forms of epistemic injustice that often take place when women from the West study women's autonomy in non-Western societies. She shows that these accounts are too often haunted by two "specters of the other woman," that is to say, two stereotypical preconceptions that Western analysis imposes on them: the "prisoner of patriarchy," that is, the woman on whom patriarchal oppression is imposed by force to the extent that she has no freedom (the woman who is forced to wear the veil, forced to marry, forced to stay inside); and the "dupe of patriarchy," or the woman who subscribes fully to patriarchal norms without seeing, when Western women would see it very clearly, the oppression that these norms establish and perpetuate.[17] A considerable literature in postcolonial, transnational, and decolonial feminist thought has established that the way in which Western feminists are embedded in imperialist power relations too often impairs their judgment regarding women from non-Western worlds.[18] The way in which submissiveness has been weaponized against Muslim women in France but also in the West in general convinces me that the possible harm created by culturalist imperialist representations is particularly acute where women's submission is concerned. In order to avoid these culturalist representations, I restrict the analysis to Western societies; most of my examples will come from France and the United States, which are the two countries in which I live and work.

Domination and Submission

There are commonly three meanings of the word "submission": it can refer to a disposition to obey, the action of submitting oneself and obeying, and the action of surrendering after a battle. Especially because of this third meaning, submission has a negative overtone and is thought of as surrendering, literally or figuratively. Contemporary debates on sadomasochism led to an attribution of a sexual connotation to "submission" and strongly bound sexual domination with sexual submission. The negative overtone of submission is not as sharp in this sexual context, but it remains.

The first difficulty one encounters when seeking to distinguish between submission and domination is the linguistic ambiguity of the verb "to submit." Contrary to the verb "to dominate" for instance, which is mostly transitive,[19] the verb "to submit" can be both transitive (to submit someone) and reflexive (to submit oneself to someone). In its transitive uses, "submit" has a similar—although slightly different—meaning than "dominate": it concerns an action conceived from the perspective of the person who accomplishes it and that consists in exerting one's power over one or more people, hence modifying their possibilities of action. One of the central uses of this verb pertains to the vocabulary of war: to submit an enemy is to succeed in dominating him enough so that he would have no other option than surrendering and placing himself under (*sub*) the orders of the victor. In this case, to submit someone is to fully dominate someone and to do so with the use of force. It is possible to dominate someone through one's knowledge, charisma, or natural authority, whereas one is only submitted by force and constraint. This understanding of the action of submitting as a subset of the action of dominating that is specific in terms of its force explains why "dominated" and "submitted" seem to mean the same thing.

Speaking, for instance, of the domination or the submission of the working class is nonetheless not equivalent. Saying that workers are dominated is to recognize that a power is exerted on them and limits, or at least modifies, their ability to act. To talk of their submission adds a negative overtone because what is then emphasized is their dependency and their obedience to the power that is exerted on them.[20] In saying that workers are dominated, one perceives them as an impersonal mass on which an arbitrary power exerts itself, whereas if their attitude is seen as submission, one repersonalizes them to a certain extent, by insisting on their behavior in the face of the domination that they are subjected to: their situation appears to be voluntary. When I write about "submission," I seek to describe the action or the situation of the person who submits, that is, who chooses, in a way, their submission. Throughout the remainder of this book, and in order to avoid any ambiguity, this is the only use of the term I will retain: submission is the action or the attitude of the person who submits.

The action of submitting oneself appears paradoxical because it is an activity in passivity: what the subject decides, whatever the degree of rationality or complexity of this decision, is to *not* be the one who decides. Of course, one can decide to submit because one has no other available choice, but in any case it is a decision, if only a decision to not act against the power exerted on oneself. In this respect, two types of will can be distinguished in submission: an active will, which would be a positive will to be submissive, or a passive will, which would be resigning oneself or not resisting the power that is exerted. In any case, one can only talk about submission when there is no active resistance to power, when the attitude or the action expresses a will of the agent. Submission is thus, at a minimum, the result of a will to not actively resist domination.

In order to understand precisely the relationship between submission and domination, it is important to see that the term "domination" is equivocal. When one talks about domination, one can refer either to a *relation*—for instance, male domination is the name commonly given to the relationship between the social group of men and the social group of women in a

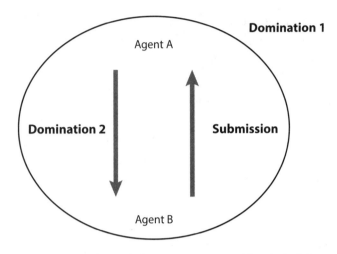

Domination as a relation (1), domination as an action (2), and submission.

patriarchal society—or to an *action*—this male domination happens through actions of domination, and acts of domestic violence are among them. A relation of domination is a vertical, hierarchical, asymmetrical relationship between at least two agents in which one agent—the one who dominates—can decisively influence the actions of the other agent—the one who is dominated. Once this difference is apparent, what submission is appears clearly: in a relation of domination (that is domination in the sense 1) between an agent A and an agent B, there can be an action of domination (in the sense 2) of A over B and an action of submission of B to A.

There can be relations of domination with no submission—this is the case when domination happens through violence and constraint—and therefore where domination in the sense 1 relies only on domination in the sense 2. In that case, there is no submission in the sense that there is no real *will* to obey from the person who obeys, since the alternative is obedience or death. A domination without submission is a domination grounded on violence and thus, by its very nature, is an unstable domination since as soon as violence disappears domination vanishes with it—contrary to a domination that would be grounded at least partly in a complicity of the dominated. It is also possible to imagine a situation in which there would be no action of domination (i.e., no domination in the sense 2) and where domination in the sense 1 would only rely on submission; this is what is commonly called voluntary submission. A possible example of this kind of submission is one in which a masochist seeks a woman who would agree to be his master, for instance, as it appears in the works of Sacher-Masoch, the Austrian writer from whose name the term "masochism" is derived. Most often, however, the relations of domination are produced by a mix of actions of domination and actions of submission.

With Beauvoir

The diagram of domination allows us to better grasp our subject: studying women's submission consists in studying the action or the situation of women when they take part, as inferiors, in a relation of domination that they do not resist. It implies looking at male domination not from the perspective of the dominants but from the perspective of those who submit *themselves*. Instead of describing women's subordination in an external and objective manner, it means wondering what it is for a woman to be a woman living in male domination and thus describing a subjective, from the bottom-up experience of domination. It means purposefully not starting from the idea that submission would be in women's nature, or against women's nature, that it would be immoral, or the sign of an oppressed false consciousness shaped by patriarchy. To the contrary, the ambition of this book is to study, without preconceptions, the submission women experience, how it manifests itself, how it is lived, and how it can be explained.

In order to do so, the argument of this book progresses through a close reading of Simone de Beauvoir's *The Second Sex*,[21] likely the most read and best-selling philosophical text of the twentieth century—probably even in the history of philosophy.[22] Yet its reception has been ambivalent: its philosophical importance began to be recognized when feminist theorists started distancing themselves from it and viewing it as outdated. The result is that the relevance of Beauvoir's analyses for understanding the current oppression of women has not received enough attention in recent years.[23] This book aims to demonstrate that the submission of women is a crucial topic for both feminism and philosophy and that Beauvoir's thinking provides deeply original, important, and relevant ways to understand it. In order to do so, this book provides a detailed philosophical analysis of *The Second Sex* to show the following:

(1) Beauvoir's conception of gender difference enables her to highlight and to historicize the relationship between femininity and submission.

(2) Beauvoir provides the first detailed account of what submission is thanks to her original appropriation of the phenomenological method.

(3) Beauvoir's theory of oppression as othering demonstrates that submission constitutes a social destiny for women to such an extent that women can even take pleasure in it.

(4) Beauvoir builds a philosophy of the body that shows that patriarchy makes women's bodies belong to men before belonging to women themselves.

(5) Beauvoir's theory of freedom explains both why women submit to men and how they could emancipate themselves.

This book is not primarily a book on Beauvoir's philosophy, but it argues that the best way to understand women's submission is to *think with Beauvoir*. Yet the depth and significance of Beauvoir's contributions cannot be fully appreciated in isolation from their intellectual context, as is always the case in philosophy. Therefore, the argument of the book leads us, at times, to discuss other philosophers with whom Beauvoir is in conversation, but only insofar as it helps our inquiry on submission. In using the philosophical analyses deployed in *The Second Sex* to understand women's submission, this book thus also aims to contribute to the philosophical scholarship on Beauvoir and to argue (against a view held by some contemporary feminist theorists) that her analyses are far from outdated and that her philosophy allows us to think more clearly about the world we live in and to make it more hospitable.[24]

2

Is Submission Feminine?
Is Femininity a Submission?

In order to understand women's submission, one must first and foremost confront the following problem: since the idea that submission is in their nature very clearly harms women, it is tempting to turn a blind eye to submission, to say that there is no such thing as female submission and that it is a sexist prejudice among many others. However, colloquial uses, classical culture, popular culture, and media representations suggest that there is something feminine in submission or submissive in femininity. Submissive men are often mocked for their lack of manliness, and the classical models of femininity are models of submission to men. So what exactly is the relationship between submission and femininity?

Are Women Masochistic?

When we hear the word "submission," the figures that commonly come to mind are the following: the submissive woman, the slave, and the defeated warrior. For the slave and the defeated warrior, this submission is the result of a physical constraint that they cannot avoid and for which they do not bear responsibility (though the warrior can be "blamed" for not being strong enough to avoid submitting).[1] In the figure of the submissive woman, on the other hand, submission appears as chosen, and the woman is thus responsible for it. Submission is then a form of consented passivity that is either the expected attitude of a respectable woman (one can think of Penelope waiting for Ulysses) or a degraded form of femininity (the one targeted, for instance, by discourses on female empowerment). When one thinks about submission as a *moral* issue—because of the voluntary and immoral renouncing of one's freedom it displays—the typical figure that comes to mind is a woman.

This conception of submission as something typically feminine is also found in the commonly held idea that women are naturally masochistic—meaning, broadly, that they like being treated badly—and that this would explain domestic violence as well as inequalities in the labor market. The falsity of such a claim has been established many times,[2] but given its prevalence, it is interesting to note how it is rooted in the theory of masochism proposed by Sigmund Freud. The problem that masochism raises for psychoanalysis is the apparent contradiction in taking pleasure from experiencing pain, especially in the sexual domain. This problem is a psychological one—that is, is it a form of perversion or of madness to take pleasure in pain?—as well as a logical one. Indeed, pleasure and pain are reciprocally defined: they are opposites and, therefore, masochism appears as a challenge to the law of noncontradiction. If there is pleasure, then there should not be pain, and vice versa. Even though pleasure taken to pain is theoretically unthinkable, doctors and psychiatrists in the nineteenth century observed, practically, the pleasure that some of their patients took in pain and attributed it to a form of perversion, partly because of the logical contradiction such symptoms manifest. Confronted with this problem, Freud wrote three texts that constitute the foundation of the psychoanalytic conception of masochism:[3] "The Sexual Aberrations" (1905), "A Child Is Being Beaten" (1919), and "The Economic Problem of Masochism" (1924).

According to Freud, masochism is a derivation, a second stage, of sadism. If, like Freud, one considers the libido as a form of the self-preservation instinct, then the masochist tendency, with its destructive proclivities, cannot make sense. This is because masochism seems precisely to go against the self-preservation instinct. In order to resolve this contradiction, Freud proposes the hypothesis of a chronological link between sadism, understood as the (sexual in some sense) desire to inflict pain, and masochism. Freud defines masochism as the reverse of sadism, but he explains it as a degraded, secondary form of sadism. In fantasies like the one he studies in "A Child Is Being Beaten," masochism appears with guilt: the child has an incestuous and sadistic desire that transforms into masochism because of the guilt he feels about this fantasy.[4] Here is the specificity of masochism: it stems from guilt. Pleasure is displaced into pain and humiliation. Masochism is therefore no longer understood as a passive aberration but rather as turning a repressed sadistic drive in upon oneself. (In the case in question, the child desires the other child to be beaten by the father because it would prove that the father does not like the other child.)

The incestuous dimension of masochistic reversal leads Freud to advance the hypothesis that the masochism of women is different from the masochism of men and that masochism is inherently *feminine*. Freud wonders about the impact of a patient's sex on the proceedings of the masochist fantasy and observes in men that "their masochistic attitude coincides with a *feminine* one,"[5] that is, that masochism is only one manifestation among others of these men's (feminine) passivity. Confronted with the lack of exact similarity between men's and women's fantasy, he concludes that "in both cases, the beating phantasy has its origin in an incestuous attachment to the father,"[6] which means that, in women, masochism would be a normal consequence of the Oedipus complex, whereas in men it is an "inverted" Oedipal attitude since it regards the father. In women, masochism is normal. In men, it is a perversion.

Freud develops this idea of a feminine character of masochism, identified with passivity, in "The Economic Problem of Masochism." He offers a typology of masochisms: three forms of masochism must be distinguished, "an *erotogenic*, a *feminine*, and a *moral* masochism."[7] Erotogenic masochism, the primary form of masochism, is the pleasure taken in experiencing pain, and it is essentially sexual. Although this masochism is presented as the original form from which the other two stem, Freud provides no explanation for it.[8] Feminine masochism is not, in Freud's view, the masochism of women; it is actually only studied in its manifestation among perverse *men*. Feminine masochism corresponds to the pleasures taken in passivity, that is, in a passive sexual and psychological position. In Freud's work, the activity/passivity pair is conceived as a fundamental opposition that is at the heart of sexual difference and participates in the definition of the masculine (as activity) and of the feminine (as passivity); therefore, the desire for passivity is identified as a feminine one. According to Freud, this masochism is the easiest to observe. This is why it is the first to be analyzed; it stems from primary masochism and it expresses a feeling of guilt.

Moral masochism is the big novelty of the Freudian conception. It consists in identifying masochistic attitudes of self-flagellation. Moral masochism manifests itself in an exacerbated feeling of guilt. Unlike the other forms of masochism, it does not have a sexual dimension—it has "loosened its connection with what we recognize as sexuality."[9] And the identity of the person who inflicts the pain does not matter to the moral masochist, since what is sought after is pain itself.

The Freudian analysis of masochism matters because it has deeply influenced the way women's behavior has been analyzed in psychology and also in social and cultural representations throughout the twentieth century. It illustrates the link between submission and femininity: the feminine masochism identified by Freud is not considered a perversion of women but a perversion of *men*. Masochism is thus normal for female subjects, whose femininity would by nature be masochistic since it is passive and rooted in a feeling of guilt. If masochism is a problem, it is only so for men, insofar as it contradicts their active nature. This identification of activity and domination with manliness, and of submission and passivity with femininity, partly explains the negative appraisal of submission: to submit oneself is to put oneself in an inferior position analogous to the inferiority of woman in relation to man.

Submission: A Feminine Virtue?

In Freud's work, the identification of masochism and femininity is grounded in a form of essentialism: there is something in women's very nature that would destine them to passivity, to a sexuality of submission and pain. Yet, in common representations as well as in classical culture, this submission does not exactly come naturally to women: the thousands of pages that theology, moral philosophy, and literature devote to prescribing submission to women and to explaining to men how to obtain it suggest that submission is a behavior that *men* consider typically feminine, or necessary to women's virtue, rather than an attitude that would be natural to them.

Some of the most important religious texts prescribe to women not only a submission to God but also a submission to their husbands. In the New Testament, in Paul's Epistle to the Ephesians, woman's submission is seen as a doubling of the submission man owes to God:

> Submitting yourselves one to another in the fear of God. Wives, submit yourselves unto your own husbands, as unto the Lord. For the husband is the head of the wife, even as Christ is the head of the church: and he is the saviour of the body. Therefore as the church is subject unto Christ, so let the wives be to their own husbands in every thing. Husbands, love your wives, even as Christ also loved the

church, and gave himself for it; That he might sanctify and cleanse it with the washing of water by the word, That he might present it to himself a glorious church, not having spot, or wrinkle, or any such thing; but that it should be holy and without blemish. So ought men to love their wives as their own bodies. He that loveth his wife loveth himself. For no man ever yet hated his own flesh; but nourisheth and cherisheth it, even as the Lord the church: For we are members of his body, of his flesh, and of his bones. For this cause shall a man leave his father and mother, and shall be joined unto his wife, and they two shall be one flesh. This is a great mystery: but I speak concerning Christ and the church. Nevertheless let every one of you in particular so love his wife even as himself; and the wife see that she reverence her husband.[10]

A specific submission of a woman to her husband is also prescribed by some sections of the Quran, of which it can be assumed that it repeats the submission that the believer owes God:

Men are the upholders and maintainers of women by virtue of that in which God has favored some of them above others and by virtue of their spending from their wealth. Therefore the righteous women are devoutly obedient, guarding in [their husbands'] absence what God has guarded. As for those from whom you fear discord and animosity, admonish them, then leave them in their beds, then strike them. Then if they obey you, seek not a way against them. Truly God is Exalted, Great.[11]

These sacred texts are open to a multiplicity of interpretations and a literal one is far from being the only or even the best reading of it.[12] However, these two excerpts illustrate the way female submission appears as a doubling of the submission of the believer to God.

In philosophy, Rousseau's recommendations regarding Sophie's education in *Émile, or, On Education* endorse the same conception of submissiveness as a virtue for women. Rousseau describes the different steps of Émile's education, each one aiming at a progressive development of his moral affections, which appear in the continuity of the awakening of his faculties. Although the reader might think, during the first four books, that Émile's education is a model for all children, this is not the case. Rousseau, in book V, addresses the education Sophie, Émile's future wife, should receive, which is also a function of her faculties. This education differs on all counts from Émile's. After purportedly establishing the existence of a natural difference between the sexes, Rousseau defends the thesis of a complementarity of the sexes, grounded in men's superiority and women's submission:

> Whether I consider the particular purpose of the fair sex, whether I observe its inclinations, whether I consider its duties, all join equally in indicating to me the form of education that suits it. Woman and man are made for one another, but their mutual dependence is not equal. Men depend on women because of their desires; women depend on men because of both their desires and needs. We would survive more easily without them than they would without us. For

them to have what is necessary to their station, they depend on us to give it to them, to want to give it to them, to esteem them worthy of it. They depend on our sentiments, on the value we set on their merit, on the importance we attach to their charms and their virtues. By the very law of nature women are at the mercy of men's judgments, as much for their own sake as for that of their children. It is not enough that they be estimable; they must be esteemed. It is not enough for them to be pretty; they must please. It is not enough for them to be temperate; they must be recognized as such. Their honor is not only in their conduct but in their reputation; and it is not possible that a woman who consents to be regarded as disreputable can ever be decent. When a man acts well, he depends only on himself and can brave public judgment; but when a woman acts well, she has accomplished only half of her task, and what is thought of her is no less important to her than what she actually is. From this it follows that the system of woman's education ought to be contrary in this respect to the system of our education. Opinion is the grave of virtue among men and its throne among women. . . .

Always justify the cares that you impose on young girls, but always impose cares on them. Idleness and disobedience are the two most dangerous defects for them and the ones least easily cured once contracted. Girls ought to be vigilant and industrious. That is not all. They ought to be constrained very early. This misfortune, if it is one for them, is inseparable from their sex, and they are never delivered from it without suffering far more cruel misfortunes. All their lives they will be enslaved to the most continual and most severe of constraints—that of the proprieties. They must first be exercised in constraint, so that it never costs them anything to tame all their caprices in order to submit them to the wills of others.[13]

Earlier in book V, Rousseau deduces, based on the sexual difference between men and women, a moral difference that makes women beings of opinion and not of reason, of submission and not of freedom. This moral difference rests on the idea that women lack reason and are therefore prey to their natural instincts; they have an unlimited sexual desire that they cannot restrain. Men's reason, in contrast, allows them to resist this desire, to sublimate it, and, through this mastery, to create a political society.

Unlike in Freud's texts, where submission is depicted as being part of woman's nature itself, in this passage, submission is not so much a result of woman's nature as it is the consequence of a point of view regarding the necessary conditions for a harmonious agreement of the sexes. For Émile to be a happy man and a happy citizen, he needs a submissive woman by his side. However, this submission seems to require a whole education to develop itself: if submission is in woman's nature, it is not at all in the same meaning of "nature." Whereas Freud understood submission as a manifestation of the psychological and almost biological nature of woman, that is, a nature in a descriptive sense, for Rousseau, submission is woman's nature in a normative sense: a woman *ought* to be submissive in order to be a woman in the full sense, that is, a companion for man. What is in question here is not woman as a female human but woman as a person who corresponds to the norms of femininity in a patriarchal society.

We can clearly see here the extent to which submission and femininity intertwine: submission is seen as the appropriate behavior of woman, the one through which a woman realizes her feminine nature, the one that fundamentally differentiates man and woman. Femininity thus has an intrinsically submissive quality and submission an intrinsically feminine one.

To Be a Woman Is to Submit

To view submission as women's nature allows classical theology, philosophy, and literature to justify social hierarchy between men and woman in making it not the result of a domination of men over woman but of a natural submission of women to men. To say women are naturally submissive implies indeed that men would have to do nothing for women to obey them and thus that they would have no responsibility in this hierarchy. This implication is very important because it make two ideas compatible: the idea that humans are born free and equal—which at first glance should make submission immoral—and the social hierarchy of the sexes. If women are not reduced to submission by men, if they choose this submission that is in their nature without men needing to dominate them, then the social superiority of men over women does not rest on an injustice.

If this way of understanding the link between femininity and submission is the most common, this link can also be a tool for a radical critique of the patriarchal organization of society, as the philosopher and legal theorist Catharine MacKinnon has shown. MacKinnon's work on gender is part of a broader systematic analysis of social and political reality, but it also has a practical dimension: she created the legal notion of sexual harassment; she has been one of the two main figures in the fight against pornography; and she obtained the recognition, in international law, of rape as a war crime in the aftermath of the war in Bosnia. In her theoretical work, she adopts a holistic perspective on the social world and seeks, through the use of social sciences and an analysis of concrete realities, to reveal the way women's oppression works. Her fundamental thesis is summarized in the following claim: "Difference is the velvet glove on the iron fist of domination. The problem is not that differences are not valued; the problem is that they are defined by power."[14] According to MacKinnon, sexual difference is the result, and not the origin, of male domination, and it serves to mask the reality of this domination. This thesis, which is counterintuitive, radical, and has very strong implications, rests on a complex argument.

SEXUALITY IS POLITICAL

The starting point of MacKinnon's argument is the following: there is a two-way relationship between the social and sexuality. The social is determined by sexuality and sexuality is determined by the social. Therefore, it is not possible to understand gender relations if one disregards their sexual dimension. MacKinnon refuses the commonly held distinction, including among feminists, between sex and gender and according to which sex would refer to the biological dimension and gender to what is socially constructed in people's identities. According to her, the social and biology are inseparable and the recourse to the sex/gender distinction contributes to the perpetuation of the idea that it would be possible at some future point to distinguish what falls under each. To this end, she claims that a political and feminist theory of sexuality is necessary. Such a theory must, in her view, "locate sexuality within a theory of gender inequality, meaning the social hierarchy of men over women," and "treat sexuality as a social construct of male power."[15]

The first theory she refutes is the idea that sexuality is natural and, therefore, that we should give ourselves over to it as much as possible and without taboo. The sexual revolution of the 1970s endorsed Freud's hypothesis that sex was repressed and that this repression was having harmful consequences on people's mental health, and, from there, was based on the idea that sex should be derepressed and people should allow themselves to fully live out their sexual desires. Against this view, MacKinnon affirms the constructed character of sexuality. She claims that sexuality is constructed by male domination and that this derepression hypothesis—MacKinnon deliberately avoids talking of sexual *liberation*—is in reality serving male sexual desires.

In her view, this is manifest, for instance, in the representation we have of sex: the normal sexual intercourse is penile penetration by a man of a woman's vagina and it ends when the man orgasms. This representation, inherited from Freud,[16] comes from the male point of view. According to MacKinnon, the general adoption of this point of view as a neutral and true one reflects the power men have over women: since men are in a dominant position, they have the possibility of defining sexuality according to what arouses them and claiming that this definition is objective. Now, the derepression hypothesis serves men's sexual interests: in affirming it is women's nature to desire frequent sexual encounters, men ensure for themselves a greater sexual availability of women. Given the power dynamic between men and women, the derepression hypothesis serves men's interests.

This refutation of the natural character of sex is predicated on a thesis that concerns both men's desire and power: "male dominance is sexual."[17] This means not only that men have sexual power over women but also—and this is a crucial contribution of MacKinnon's thought—that dominance is at the heart of men's sexuality just as much as sexuality is at the heart of their dominance. According to MacKinnon, pornography shows that what sexually arouses men is not so much sex itself or penetration but the power that manifests itself in it. Quantitative data on men's reaction to pornography indicate that what generates and maintains men's arousal over time is violence against women.[18] The data are particularly interesting when used to examine the evolution of the standards of mainstream pornography toward an increasing amount of physical and symbolic violence (BDSM, gangbangs, bukkake, etc.). From this, MacKinnon concludes that hierarchy and power, that is, dominance over women, more than sex itself, are what men value in sexuality.

The central character of dominance in men's sexuality leads to women being viewed only as objects for men's sexual satisfaction, objects that are to be dominated in sexual intercourse. There is thus a sexual domination of men over women. But this domination is not limited to a sexual sphere that is conceived as separated from the rest of the social world: the sexual domination of men over women structures the social world in its entirety. If what MacKinnon calls "hierarchy" (unequal power relations) is what arouses men—that is, if men are in a social position that allows them to enforce their desires—and if gender, understood as what distinguishes men and women, is an axis of social hierarchy, then gender must be understood as the social manifestation of men's appetite for domination.

THE SOCIAL AND SEXUAL CONSTRUCTION OF GENDER

The challenge to the conception of sexuality as natural and naturally good thus allows us to understand the two-way relation between sexuality and social organization and, therefore, the way that male domination determines sexual difference. Indeed, the analysis of the derepression hypothesis shows that the social power of men over women shapes sexuality according to men's interests, so that "normal" sexuality is the one that corresponds to men's desires. The real originality of MacKinnon's work consists in showing that the relation does not stop there: the sexuality that represents men's interests is also presented as natural and valued for its natural character. Gender difference is based on and structured by men's sexual interests, but the way those interests are naturalized—through the idea of sexuality as natural, ahistorical, and asocial—conceals that structuring process and its ideological dimension. The gendered distribution of roles structures the difference between men and women in the social world. Men are the people who sexually dominate; women are those who sexually submit:

> Male power takes the social form of what men as a gender want sexually, which centers on power itself, as socially defined. Masculinity is having it; femininity is not having it.

Masculinity precedes male as femininity precedes female and male sexual desire defines both. Specifically, "woman" is defined by what male desire requires for arousal and satisfaction and is socially tautologous with "female sexuality" and "the female sex." In the permissible ways a woman can be treated, the ways that are socially considered not violations but appropriate to her nature, one finds the particulars of male sexual interests and requirements.[19]

Male and female are created through the erotization of dominance and submission. The man/woman difference and the dominance/submission dynamic define each other. This is the social meaning of sex and the distinctively feminist account of gender inequality.[20]

The thesis of these two excerpts is a strong one: it implies that there is nothing natural and that everything is socially constructed. This thesis falls under the category of strong social constructionism. It ascribes a central position to sexuality and refutes any role of biology in shaping sex differences. MacKinnon makes the radical claim that biological differences between the sexes do not play a role in the difference between men and women.[21] When it is usually taken for granted that the masculine and the feminine are defined from the characteristics— and especially the physical ones—of men and women (that is, that what is linked to the physical or biological characteristics of men is commonly seen as masculine), MacKinnon claims that the masculine/feminine distinction precedes the distinction between men and women. The distinction between masculine and feminine is the product of male domination and relies on a relationship of mutual determination between the social and the sexual. The circularity of this relationship makes it difficult to explain in a linear way, but overall it proceeds along the following lines: male domination comes from sexuality; it inscribes itself in the social; its inscription in the social nourishes people's fantasies in return and, therefore, sexuality, thus reinforcing its valorization of domination, which then reinforces gender hierarchy in the social world.

This hypothesis is not designed to elucidate the origin of male domination but to explain its permanence and how it works. MacKinnon recognizes, in another text, that originally one sphere must be anterior to the other. She thus assumes that men originally dominated women through force.[22] This hypothesis is not central, however: MacKinnon is first and foremost a legal theorist, and her analysis of sexual difference aims to highlight an insufficiency of law.[23] She essentially seeks to shed light on the systematic character of women's oppression as women and on the way this oppression perpetuates itself.

SUBMISSION DEFINES FEMININITY

According to MacKinnon, the difference between man and woman is based on the opposition of dominance and submission: individuals who dominate are called "men," and ones who submit are called "women." Therefore, submission defines femininity. MacKinnon does not confine herself to saying men's power over women constructs the difference between masculinity and femininity. This thesis is commonly held by feminists, radical or not. She claims, in a more radical way, that dominance and submission are the attitudes from which gender difference is built. In particular, men's power over women allows them to define the difference between men and women by what arouses them. They can thus define themselves by their power and define women by the attitude they want women to have toward them. Indeed, it is not, I believe, accidental that MacKinnon uses the term "submission" rather than "subordination."[24] Subordination is the objective consequence of domination over someone. Women, for instance, have traditionally been subordinated to their husbands through the marriage contract. It is not this objective pair of notions, domination and subordination, that grounds sexual difference. What is feminine is not only to not have power, but to not be able to have this power and to recognize it. Submission, according to MacKinnon, is the attitude men sexually desire of women. Pornography, in MacKinnon's view, reveals men's desire. And it shows that submission consists, on the one hand, in women's sexual objectification—that is, their subordination to such an extent that they lose their quality of subject to become mere objects of pleasure[25]—and, on the other hand, in a form of recognition of men's sexual domination.

From Freud to MacKinnon, by way of Rousseau, one thing is clear: there is something intrinsically feminine in submission and intrinsically submissive in femininity. However, whether female submission is understood as natural, prescribed, or constructed, one thing is missing in these approaches: they are all, in their own way, interested in femininity as a set of social norms rather than in women themselves. And, in this respect, they obscure the difference between the descriptive and the normative dimensions of their theses. Is this femininity that submission grounds the femininity of all women? Of some women? Is it possible to be a woman without being submissive? The issue at stake, then, is to precisely identify the nature of this apparent close relationship between submission, femininity, and women's ordinary life—a problem that cannot be resolved by the apparent contradiction between a natural submission and a constructed one. It is through a refusal of this alternative of essentialism and strong constructionism that Simone de Beauvoir, in *The Second Sex*, helps us to solve this puzzle.

3

Womanhood as a Situation

In the previous chapter, we established that submission and femininity are conceived as intrinsically connected. Be it in religious and philosophical texts grounded in the idea of a natural difference between men and women that would justify women's submission, or in radical feminist views like MacKinnon's, femininity is conceived as inseparable from submission, and submission is seen as a feminine behavior. As we noted, one of the main issues in understanding the relationship between femininity and submission is therefore determining whether there is something *natural* in female submission—that is to say, whether it is in the nature or in the essence of women to be submissive.

Simone de Beauvoir devotes *The Second Sex* to the question of what a woman is, and her response to this question allows us to understand what submission is, how submission and femininity are connected, and ultimately why women submit to men. Beauvoir responds to the question "What is a woman?" in a very subtle manner, avoiding both the essentialist pitfall and the constructivist one. According to her, there is no immutable essence of woman, yet it is wrong to say that nothing but the name that is given to them differentiates women and men. Women are the individuals that are in a certain *situation*.

Defining womanhood as a situation is Beauvoir's first step in showing that there is something feminine in submission, but not because women are naturally submissive. Submission is not a nature, but it appears to women as a *destiny*: to be a woman is to be in a situation where submission appears as one's destiny. It is to be a person to whom submission is prescribed, from the outside. The force of the social prescription is such that it is hard to escape from it. But it doesn't follow that submission would be natural or inevitable. In fact, seeing submission as the social norm prescribed to women means that the close relationship between femininity and submission is not inevitable, that it must be seen as the result of historical power relations, and therefore that it can change.

Sexual Difference Is Not a Matter of Essences

As we have seen, female submission has historically been conceived as the result of women's nature. This conception is grounded in the assumption that men and women are naturally different and that a submissive character is one of the traits inherent in human nature. We have also seen that there are good reasons to believe that such a conception is wrong and harmful to women. Yet the intuition that men and women are in fact different is strong. The conception of gender difference proposed by Beauvoir in *The Second Sex* refutes essentialism while recognizing the intuition that gender differences exist and, as such, is the first step to understanding what exactly the relationship is between womanhood and submission.

The central problem *The Second Sex* aims to address is what philosophers since Socrates have called an essence question because it examines the essence or nature of a concept—the question "What is a woman?" Yet Beauvoir responds to it in a way that rejects essentialism (the idea that women have a *nature* or an essence).

A PHILOSOPHICAL QUESTION

As she recounts in her memoirs, Beauvoir considered *The Second Sex* a preamble to her autobiographical work to come. As she finds herself struggling to write her autobiography, she realizes in a discussion with Sartre[1] that analyzing her femininity is the necessary prerequisite to any autobiographical enterprise. She thus decides that before writing anything about herself and her life, she must answer this question, fundamentally philosophical in its form: "What is a woman?"

The problem that such a question raises when applied to "woman" is that it seems to substantiate the idea of a feminine nature. When Socrates asks, "What is virtue?" he seeks a definition that would manifest the intrinsic nature of virtue. (In ancient Greek, the question "What is X?" questions the *eidos* of X, and *eidos* can be translated as "nature" or "essence.") Looking for a nature or an essence, when applied to the concept of "woman," seems to lead to an essentialist position: there would be a feminine essence that would be distinct from a masculine one. The way Beauvoir phrases the central question of her book, as early as the first page of the introduction—in addition to the fact that throughout *The Second Sex* Beauvoir talks about "the woman" instead of "women" for instance—could lead one to believe that Beauvoir assumes the existence of a female nature and that she is an essentialist and claims that there is an essential difference between man and woman. But essentialism, when applied to sexual difference, is problematic for many reasons. One in particular is important for us and for Beauvoir: essentialism has historically been used to justify male dominance through the idea that men's nature makes them dominant and women's nature makes them submissive. Therefore, essentialism is at the root of the association between submission and femininity, which itself has been an obstacle to women's liberation[2]—and Beauvoir recognized this.

AGAINST ESSENTIALISM

Although, intuitively, we could think that any response to the question "What is a woman?" would tell us what the essence of woman is, Beauvoir asks this "essence question" without giving it an essentialist answer. To understand how she rejects essentialism, it is useful to distinguish between different types of essentialism.

When one talks about sexual difference, the first and most evident essentialism that comes to mind is biological essentialism—that is, the idea that there are sufficiently significant biological differences between the sexes to establish a masculine and a feminine essence. Beauvoir does not reject the idea of biological differences between males and females in the human species, but she rejects biological determinism, the idea that biological differences would determine men and women and set for them an inescapable destiny. One of her arguments against biological determinism is the following: "Not every female human being is necessarily a woman; she must take part in this mysterious and endangered reality known as femininity."[3] Biological differences between human males and females are not enough to account for the division between men and women in human societies and even less so for the almost mystical dimension bestowed upon femininity.

A second type of essentialism rejected by Beauvoir is metaphysical essentialism, namely the idea that an object or a being possesses a certain property or quality by virtue of which it is what it is. This is precisely the essentialism of Socrates and Plato. For example, the essence of a triangle is to be a three-sided polygon. Applied to sex difference, metaphysical essentialism implies that there would be a real essence of sexes, independent of social construction. There would be some properties of the woman that all women, and only women, would have and that would allow one to define the essence of a woman as clearly as the three sides define the triangle. Such an essentialism has an ahistorical dimension: it assumes that metaphysical essences have a reality that does not change over time. Thus, as the myth of the Eternal feminine holds it, there would always have been something called femininity, it would have remained the same throughout history, and it would belong to all women and only women. Beauvoir relies on the challenge of this ahistoricism by what she calls "the biological and social sciences" to reject such a fixed essence of femininity: if femininity has not been exactly the same over the centuries, this means femininity is not a fixed nature. As ahistoricism is inseparable from this metaphysical essentialism, the falseness of ahistoricism is sufficient to reject the eternal feminine.

Lastly, she rejects linguistic essentialism, namely the idea that everyone is referring to the same thing when they use the word "woman," in showing that this term is used descriptively as well as normatively. When newspapers complain about the "disappearance of woman" in order to complain about the decline of a certain understanding of femininity, they do not refer to the same meaning of the word as when the word "woman" is used in statistical studies to refer to the gender of the people surveyed. In one case, woman is a descriptive category in a classification. In the other, the word refers to a social norm, the social norm of femininity.

Against all the forms of essentialism, Beauvoir claims at the beginning of her book: "Certainly, woman like man is a human being."[4] How is it then that she devotes almost eight hundred pages to answering to the question "What is a woman?"

Femininity as Social Construction?

Beauvoir warns as much against essentialism as against nominalism—the idea that "women are, among human beings, merely those who are arbitrarily designated by the word 'woman.'"[5] She rejects essentialism without endorsing the idea, defended by MacKinnon, that only social organization explains the difference that we see between a group of men and a group of women. On the contrary, according to her, such a claim amounts to blindness. Pretending that nothing differentiates men and women except for the word used to name them is tantamount to being unaware of the reality of the social order and of the existence of real, concrete differences between men and women. Walking along the street, she says, one sees clearly that there are women and there are men. Even if she does not mention them, one could add that the existence of gender-nonconforming people does not go against this evidence: it is precisely because some people are not easily and straightforwardly ascribable to one category or another that a part of the population rejects them as *queer*.[6] In the face of this evidence of sex difference[7] in the social order, one must hold together both the fact that women are human beings and the fact that sexual difference is blindingly obvious. Therefore, according to Beauvoir, it is necessary to ask the essence question "What is a woman?" not so much because there is a feminine essence that is distinct from the masculine one but because sex difference is one of the crucial components of what she calls the "situation."[8]

Before analyzing her use of the concept of "situation," it is important to understand that in rejecting essentialism, as well as nominalism, Beauvoir endorses an original position in the feminist debate, occurring long after the release of *The Second Sex*, between essentialism and constructionism. She claims that there is neither a feminine essence nor a femininity that would be sheer social construction. The most famous sentence of *The Second Sex*, "one is not born, but rather becomes, woman," led some of Beauvoir's readers, first and foremost Judith Butler, the philosopher whose work gave birth to gender studies, to see Beauvoir as the precursor of the recognition of the socially constructed nature of gender and of the arbitrary link that society established between sex and gender.[9] If one is not born a woman, it must be because there is no determinism linked to biological sex. And if one becomes a woman nonetheless, it must be that society is responsible for this difference. However, Beauvoir's claim is more nuanced. She writes:

> One is not born, but rather becomes, woman. No biological, psychological, economic destiny defines the figure that the human female takes on in society; it is civilization as a whole that elaborates this intermediary product between the male and the eunuch that is called feminine.[10]

Beauvoir refuses to restrain herself to adopting only one interpretative framework of sex difference, be it drawn from biology, psychoanalysis, or economics (by which she meant Marxism). On the contrary, she affirms that sex difference must be considered as a whole, without presuming that one framework would be better or sufficient to account for it. In particular, Beauvoir gives biology a completely different status than the one Butler gives it. Admittedly, like Butler, she rejects the hypothesis of a biological determinism. However, she takes biology very seriously—*The Second Sex* is the most complete review of the biology of sex difference at the time of its publication, though a great deal of its biological analyses are now outdated given the progress of developmental biology since 1949. She devotes the first chapter of the book to "biological data." In this chapter, she does not refute the idea of a biological binarity—according to her, there are males and females in the human species, with clear differences. Nor does she deny that biological differences between males and females have an impact on the social difference between men and women.

These differences do have an impact on the way the difference between men and women is perceived in society, but they do not definitively ground this difference:[11] there is biological *data*, but they in no way create an inescapable *destiny*.

In this, Beauvoirian philosophy is truly existentialist. According to existentialism, human beings are those whose specific characteristic is that their existence precedes—logically and chronologically—their essence. It is the way humans live their life that determines who they are, not a predetermined essence. Therefore, what a woman is does not come from a preexisting essence but from the way she lives in the world. The social dimension of human interactions is much more important than biology in sexual difference, and only this social dimension confers a meaning to biological differences. Certain biological differences are meaningful while others have no impact on the definition of femininity;[12] women's essence is shaped by their existence in the world.

The difference between Beauvoir's and Butler's positions stems from a disagreement on social construction. When Butler claims that gender is nothing more than a social construction—a thesis known as strong social constructionism— this claim is implicitly inseparable from the postmodern idea that there is no reality independent from our practices or our language[13] and that the notions of truth and reality are only fictions employed by dominants to conceal their power. Yet when Beauvoir writes "one is not born, but rather becomes, woman," she does not make such an inference. First, she rejects biological differences as determining sexual difference in the name of the greater importance of social reality, but she does not deny sexual differences. Second, and more importantly, she does not conclude from this that sex difference would not be real or true: she only claims it should be studied as something socially situated.

Situation and Sexual Difference

The concept of "situation" is key to overcoming the opposition between essentialism (there is an essence of femininity that precedes women's existence) and nominalism (women are the people that are called women). This concept allows for the recognition both that women are assigned a social destiny, a norm that preexists them and conditions their existence, and that they can transcend this social destiny. This does not mean that women can, or should, overcome this destiny by overlooking it as purely contingent—their situation is truly one of inferiority—but that their freedom allows them to transform and escape it. Beauvoir writes in the introduction to *The Second Sex*:

> When an individual or a group of individuals is kept in a situation of inferiority, the fact is that he or they *are* inferior. But it is about the scope of the verb *to be* that we need to be clear; bad faith entails giving it a substantial value, when in fact it has the Hegelian dynamic meaning: *to be* is to have become, to have been made as one manifests oneself; yes, women in general *are* today inferior to men, that is their situation opens fewer possibilities to them: the question is whether this state of affairs must continue.[14]

The concept of "situation" both describes the reality of women's inferiority in relation to men and historicizes it, that is, it shows there is nothing natural and therefore fixed in this inferiority. Against a platonic essentialism that would present women's inferiority as natural and fixed, Beauvoir claims the necessity to conceive of this inferiority as *historical*, as the result of a historical process. To say that women are inferior does not mean that it has always been the case or that it will always be so. Historicizing women's inferiority allows, on the one hand, to think of its past—to think of it as the result of an oppression, as something that has happened—and, on the other hand, to think of its future—that is, the possibility of women's emancipation.

AGAINST SARTRE

Although one of the most commonly held misconceptions about *The Second Sex* is that Beauvoir, as Sartre's romantic partner and first disciple (she was commonly called the Great Sartrean at the time), is merely applying Sartrean philosophy to women's issues, it is very clear from the first pages of the book that Beauvoir's concept of "situation" is radically different from the one Sartre develops in *Being and Nothingness*.

According to Sartre, every individual is in a certain situation, but this situation can and should be overcome—what he calls "transcended." In *Being and Nothingness*, published in 1943, six years prior to *The Second Sex*, the concept of "situation" is intrinsically connected to those of freedom and "facticity." According to Sartre, human beings are fundamentally free, whatever the initial conditions of their existence. This is a metaphysical claim and not a practical one: Sartre is not exactly arguing that we are all practically free to do whatever we want, but, for Sartre, the specific characteristic of human beings is their freedom in the sense that, unlike a paper cutter for instance, they do not have a fixed purpose and destiny. This does not mean that the social, historical, and economic conditions in which the individual finds himself do not exist or should not be taken into account; but it means they are *contingent*. They are what he calls a "facticity," which is a given without reason, a contingency that human freedom must overcome.[15] Situation, according to Sartre, is therefore the pure contingency of our existence, the only thing we do not choose, the only given, against which freedom must be exerted and to which freedom must give a meaning. The fact that I am born somewhere, of certain parents, and that I was raised in a certain way does not say anything about who I am, as I am free to transform and overcome these facts. Freedom is a negation of the facticity of situation. For Sartre, people who are failing to recognize that they are free to overcome their contingent facticity and use this facticity to justify themselves—in saying that they have to act a certain way because they are poor, or rich, or born into a certain family instead of recognizing they are free to choose the way they act—are acting in an inauthentic manner and are displaying what Sartre calls bad faith.[16]

Beauvoir disagrees deeply with Sartre's account of freedom. For her, authenticity consists in recognizing we are in a certain situation and that this situation shapes the ways in which we can use our freedom. Sartre and Beauvoir's disagreement is recounted both in her first philosophical essays and in her memoirs. In *The Prime of Life*, the part of her memoirs covering her life from the end of 1920s until the end of World War II, her disagreement with Sartre on the idea that situation is a pure facticity from which the free individual must extract himself and on the correlated idea that the individual is morally responsible for this extraction no matter the situation in which he finds himself is thus described:

> During the days that followed we discussed certain specific problems, in particular the relationship between "situation" and freedom. I maintained that from the angle of freedom as Sartre defined it—that is, an active transcendence of some given context rather than mere stoic resignation—not every situation was equivalent: what sort of transcendence could a woman shut up in a harem achieve? Sartre replied that even such a cloistered existence could be lived in several quite different ways. I stuck to my point for a long time, and in the end made only a token submission. At the bottom, I was right. But to defend my attitude I should have had to abandon the plane of individual, and therefore idealistic, morality on which we had set ourselves.[17]

At the end of *The Prime of Life*, Beauvoir presents the war—especially the war insofar as it constituted the experience of an inextinguishable presence of death for her—as the reason for a sort of philosophical conversion: while Sartre and she bathed until then in their detached, apolitical individualism, the war leads her to reject the idea of an individual independent from the world in which she finds herself. Every individual is situated,[18] and fully understanding that necessitates "committing"[19] to society. This conversion appears clearly in *The Ethics of Ambiguity*, the philosophical text she published right after the end of the war. This text is adorned with more or less explicit references to Heidegger and revisits her disagreement with Sartre on facticity. Beauvoir takes a strong, albeit implicit, stand against the asocial conception of freedom developed by Sartre in *Being and Nothingness*. She thus writes: "The Black slave of the eighteenth century, the Muslim woman locked up in the bottom of a harem have no instrument, be it in thought or by astonishment or anger, which permits them to attack the civilization which oppresses them."[20] According to Beauvoir, contrary to Sartre's thesis, everyone is always in a certain economic and social situation that shapes the form that their freedom can take. Far from being accidental and contingent, their situation demonstrates that they do not exist outside a world that they are at the same time shaping by their very presence. And a paradigmatic example of this is the fact that being a woman in the world is not the same thing as being a man.

THE INDIVIDUAL AND THE SOCIAL WORLD

This Beauvoirian concept of "situation" is crucial for understanding the problem of women's submission because it shows that gender shapes how individuals are in the world and what they can do, without assuming that gender has to do with nature: being a woman is different from being a man not because there is an essential difference between human males and human females but because men and women are not situated in the same way in society and thus cannot exert their freedom in the same way.

More precisely, the concept of "situation" provides a way to understand the problem of submission in its complexity because instead of focusing solely on the individual (as in the essentialist explanation) or on the society (as in strong constructionism), it articulates the role of the individual and the role of the society. Indeed, to understand how female submission functions, one must hold together two levels, the one of the individual, who makes choices and behaves in certain ways, and the one of society, which prescribes certain behaviors to individuals and shapes their preferences. When Beauvoir, during the war, refutes the individualist position of Sartre and favors the thesis of the situated individual, she precisely holds these two levels together.

To reach such a complexity in her analysis, Beauvoir appropriates some elements of Heidegger's ontology as it is laid out in *Being and Time*. Beauvoir's memoirs provide the grounds to believe that Heidegger played a much bigger role in her philosophical ideas than usually recognized. She considers him the philosopher who convinced her to abandon her prewar individualism:

> The further I went, the more I diverged from Hegel, without ever losing my admiration for him. I knew already that in the very marrow of my being I was bound up with my contemporaries; now I was learning that this dependent condition carried a complementary burden of responsibility. Heidegger had convinced me that "human reality" is accomplished and expressed in each separate living being. Conversely, each person also commits and jeopardizes this "reality" as a whole. The individual's concept of himself, either as a man among men or an ant on an anthill, will depend on whether his society is aiming at the achievement of freedom, or content to endure passive bondage; yet each of us has the power to challenge that collective decision, to

reject or confirm it. Every day I experienced this ambiguous solidarity. In this occupied France, the mere fact of breathing implied consent in oppression. Not even suicide would have freed me, it would have sanctioned my defeat; my salvation was bound up with that of the whole country. But this situation that was forced on me, my remorse had shown me that I contributed to creating it. The individual doesn't resorb itself in the circumambient universe: while coping with it, he acts on it, if only by his very immobility.[21]

Beauvoir's reading of Heidegger, together with her experience of war and occupation, leads her to think anew on the questions of submission, choice, and responsibility, and to refuse both an individualist approach and a structural and impersonal one. The consent to oppression she explores here and that she confronts in *The Second Sex* is better understood when one grasps the relationship between the individual and the world in the way Heidegger does.

This is not the place to summarize *Being and Time*, but Heidegger's work is often misconstrued and seen as obscure because of the technicality of its prose. However, a few core ideas that he develops can help us understand how Beauvoir will explain women's submission. What is at stake for Heidegger is to understand what "being" is. In his view, traditional metaphysics lost sight of this question in focusing on entities, on what is, instead of interrogating what being is. To avoid this error, he proposes to start from the particular being that he calls Dasein and to ask the question of what "being" is from there. The Dasein, literally in German the "being here," and what Beauvoir and the French readers of Heidegger at the time translate as "human reality," is the human being apprehended in a specific manner, as the only being able to ask themselves what it means for them to be the being that they are.[22]

The analysis of Dasein and their place in the world matters for Beauvoir because through it Heidegger radically breaks with a classical idea of philosophy: that the individual preexists the world and creates it. The common way of presenting the relationship between the individual and the world is to describe the individual as first acquiring a consciousness of herself, and then encountering other people and the world in general. For Heidegger, there is not first an isolated individual, who gives sense to their own world, then to others, then to the world in general. For the Dasein, the world is as primordial as they are themselves. There is not on the one hand the subject and on the other hand a world made of objects. The Dasein inhabits the world; they are absorbed and involved in the world. The world is not something exterior to the Dasein but a whole in which all things are in a relationship of involvement or commitment with each other: in their daily ordinary activity, the Dasein knows the things insofar as they use them and as they appear to them as being part of a totality of significations. For instance, a nail has a meaning as a nail only because it is found in a workshop, in which there are a hammer, planks, and also a carpenter. The most ordinary way of being for the Dasein consists in being in the world in a non-reflexive way, only because they evolve in this world and use tools that bear meaning in relation to the totality of the world.

This first idea—that the Dasein cannot be thought as primordially out of the world in which they find themselves, or at least that the abstraction of the world in this manner does not correspond to the way human beings are primordially in the world—is very important for Beauvoir's understanding of sex difference. It implies that sex difference will have to be thought in terms of both its social and its individual dimension: every individual arrives in a world in which sex difference already exists, and at the same time, every individual, by his or her sheer existence, will have an impact on what we understand collectively as sex difference. Moreover, this conception implies that it is impossible to think the individual before sex difference: every female person is born into a world in which being a woman already means something.

LIVING WITH OTHERS

One crucial consequence of this interdependence of Dasein and the world is that the individual is not first isolated and then socialized with others: according to Heidegger, the Dasein is always with others. There is not first my world then the world; there is only one world and it is shared with others. Contrary to Sartre's individualism, in everyday life, according to Heidegger, one is not first an "I" that will then encounter others; there is no primordial time in which the individual would be alone before meeting others. In daily life, in work, one encounters others. They are always already there.

This being-with (Heidegger calls it *Mitsein*, and Beauvoir uses this German term seven times in *The Second Sex*, thus very explicitly acknowledging her use of Heidegger's ontology) has a decisive consequence in Beauvoirian philosophy: Heidegger conceives of the relationship with others first as harmonious or at worst neutral. Most of the time, the relationship with others is a neutral one—the Dasein passes others, crosses them, or is indifferent to them—or a positive one when one is trying to help others. The relationship with others is not conceived, as, for instance, in Hegel, as a conflict of individuals. It is not even really a relationship; it consists in inhabiting the world together. This idea is also crucial for understanding sexual difference: sexual difference is not first understood as a form of conflictuality, as the dominance of men over women, for instance. Rather, it belongs to these facts that are so obvious that we do not think about them: one lives in a world in which some individuals are men, others are women, and we do not even think about this division. This division appears as an object for reflection only from the moment it causes issues—for instance, when it creates unjust inequalities or excludes people. From there, one understands that it is not possible to settle for an individualist approach: the individual is not alone in the world and he does not preexist the world. But a problem remains: How should we understand the influence of the world on the individual? For Heidegger, as for Beauvoir, the answer is to be found in the idea of social norms.

SOCIAL NORMS

The world in which the Dasein lives is familiar to them;[23] they know how to behave in it. This does not mean that the Dasein cannot freely act, but it means that every human being is in a certain way determined by their situation, that is, by their place in the world. The individual is determined by the world in which they live because this world is a significant whole, unified by social norms. For instance, because I grew up in France, I know, in a non-reflexive manner, that I will greet my friends by kissing them on both cheeks and not by hugging them. I also know that when I am a pedestrian at a carless crossing I can walk across the street even if the traffic light does not allow it. These constitute a non-reflexive knowledge; I simply integrated possible or recommended behaviors that would be different had I grown up in the United States. According to Heidegger, our daily behaviors function mostly thanks to these norms that we adopted without even thinking about them and that continuously orient us. In that regard, the world as a set of social norms, of things we can or cannot do, preexists every Dasein. At the same time, a Dasein is needed to make this world and these norms appear: it is because I act according to these social norms—whether in conforming to them or in opposing them—that they are social norms and the world is a whole.

One of the ways these norms function comes from the fact that Dasein sees in other people's behavior a norm of their action. In everyday life, individuals act without reflection, on the basis of what "one" does in a given situation. To return to my previous example, when I see a friend, I kiss her on both cheeks to greet her because that is what other people do and, therefore, is considered what "one" does, or what is done, as a social norm. Of course, there can be something problematic in this "one" insofar as it incites the individual to conform to social norms rather than to interrogate the grounds of their action. But, at the same time, the "one" is a source of intelligibility: the social norm allows us to understand the meaning of other people's behaviors, insofar as it prescribes an appropriate way to be in the world,[24] in the light of which everyone's behavior will be understandable.

To refer to the "one" is thus not a form of bad faith; it is not a lie to oneself in which the individual would take refuge behind customs to avoid taking responsibility. No one escapes this way of being. Contrary to Sartre's view according to which the subject is free and falls into bad faith when he refuses his freedom and indulges in his facticity, for Heidegger, Dasein's primordial experience is the experience of a relationship with other entities and other Daseins on the mode of cohabitation, a cohabitation ruled by social norms. Dasein, by the very fact that they grew up somewhere, among others, possess an "already there" understanding of the world. There is no decision or choice made by Dasein here: they always arrive in a world that already has a meaning. This does not mean that Dasein is completely determined by these norms, but it means that any interpretation of the world, any action of theirs, will detach itself on the background that is this public interpretation. According to Heidegger, Dasein has good reasons to understand their world as having the form of a social destiny, of a life already publicly interpreted by the world in which they live.

FEMININITY, SITUATION, AND SOCIAL NORMS

This brief overview of Beauvoir's use of Heidegger shows that when Beauvoir recognizes the human being as situated, she affirms that we are in a world in which our being always already has a meaning and a norm. But this meaning and this norm are products of history and not a fixed nature. It means that a woman cannot pretend she is simply a human being, since in this world sexual difference exists and structures the possibilities of action. Beauvoir illustrates this with an example of a young political activist she saw at a Trotskyite meeting, who was stirring up the crowd in an aggressive manner, as male political activists do. But Beauvoir shows that this woman, who thinks she is behaving like a man, is doing so to impress the man she loves, which is a typically feminine thing to do. Her inauthenticity, her bad faith, derives from the fact that she pretends that her way of acting is not shaped by her situation when she is actually behaving exactly in the way that is prescribed to women by social norms since she behaves as she does out of love.[25] Against Sartre's idea that all subjects find themselves situated in a more or less accidental way, in a world exterior to them and toward which they can and must affirm a form of independence, for Beauvoir, to say that individuals are situated is recognizing that they are in the world, in the sense that they do not exist outside the world which, at the same time, they shape by their very presence.

This is not to say that the essentialist perspective would be more authentic. Beauvoir refutes the hypothesis that the woman, the Jew, and the Black are defined by immutable and natural characters, but she ascribes their character to a *situation* that they have to recognize before they can try to overcome it:

> The fact is that every concrete human being is always uniquely situated. To reject the notions of the eternal feminine, the black soul, or the Jewish character is not to deny that there are today Jews, blacks, or women: this denial is not a liberation for those concerned but an inauthentic flight. Clearly, no woman can claim without bad faith to be situated beyond her sex.[26]

Indeed, Beauvoir does not solely use elements of the Heideggerian understanding of being-in-the-world; she introduces elements of Marxist analysis in her concept of "situation." Unlike Sartre, Beauvoir started reading Marx and Marxist authors in the early 1930s,[27] and she conceived then the necessity of a philosophy concretely anchored in the social world. Yet, as she explains in *The Ethics of Ambiguity*, she struggles with the way in which Marxism negates individual freedom in the name of the social structure.[28] The Beauvoirian concept of "situation" functions, therefore, in a way that holds together the individualism of existentialism with the care for the structural issues of Marxism. Through this concept of "situation," Beauvoir shows that any existential subject lives its singularity in the context of social conditions. Beauvoir's desire to avoid a solipsist vision of existentialism leads her to grant a considerably greater importance to the economic and social structures than to individual existential considerations to understand what humans, and women in particular, go through. She thus writes in *The Ethics of Ambiguity*:

> We have already pointed out that certain adults can live in the universe in the serious in good faith, for example, those who are denied all instruments of escape, those who are enslaved, or mystified. The less economic and social circumstances allow an individual to act upon the world, the more this world appears to him as given. This is the case of women who inherit a long tradition of submission.[29]

The concept of "situation," therefore, does not refer to the simple facticity in which the subject finds herself—the fact of being born somewhere, of a certain family—but to the social and economic structures in which individuals find themselves. The consequence of this is that bad faith, understood as individuals' tendency to use their situation as a justification for their shortcomings, is not a radical moral fault like it is in Sartre's view.[30] True bad faith consists, on the contrary, in the refusal to recognize that we are in a certain situation, in which sex difference, as well as skin color, for instance, is significant. To be free is not to oppose facticity but to recognize it in order to position oneself with regard to it. If the situation is contingent in the sense that it is not chosen by the subject, she cannot settle for simply denying it if she wants to exert her freedom. Denying it would be a sort of lie to oneself that would impair action.

It thus becomes clear how Beauvoir can reject the myth of the Eternal Feminine or more broadly the idea of a feminine nature—that is, claim the socially constructed character of femininity—without considering that this construction would imply that sexual difference or femininity would not be real. Since any individual is always in a world that is already interpreted, already structured by norms that give a certain meaning to the individual's properties—sex, age, skin color—the individual cannot shape herself otherwise than with regard to these norms, be it in agreement, in opposition, or in complacency. In Beauvoir's philosophy, there is no way to conceive of the individual outside of their social situation. The fact that sexual difference is blindingly obvious for everyone demonstrates that femininity has a reality for individuals even though—and that's Beauvoir position—it would only be the product of human history. Applied to sexual difference, the concept of "situation" thus allows us to understand the necessity of studying sexual difference in order to understand what it is to be a woman,

without a recourse to essentialism or strong social constructionism. The first obvious answer to the question "What is a
woman?" is grounded in the ordinary and social experience
that we have of sexual difference:

> One only has to walk around with her eyes opened to see
> that humanity is split in two categories of individuals with
> manifestly different clothes, faces, bodies, smiles, move-
> ments, interests, and occupations; these differences are
> perhaps superficial; perhaps they are destined to disappear.
> What is certain is that for the moment, they exist in a strik-
> ingly obvious way.[31]

Beauvoir thus affirms the existence of difference without adopting an essentialist position. She clearly rejects a mythical or biological explanation of sexual difference and, at the same time,
highlights the reality of this difference and its importance in
women's situation. Beauvoir claims that it would be a form of
bad faith for a woman to want to "be situated beyond her sex"[32]
because sex difference belongs to the social norms that organize
the world into which everyone is born.

Femininity, Situation, and Destiny

Showing that being a woman is being in a certain situation
implies examining (1) what this situation means, how it is built
from the perspective of men; and (2) how this situation is lived.
And the way this situation is lived is that it is lived as a destiny.
Heidegger deliberately places himself on an ontological level,
in focusing on Dasein, a human being insofar as it is stripped
from all facticity. On the contrary, Beauvoir orients her inquiry

toward the sheer facticity that sex, namely female sex, entails. Her goal is to analyze women's situation in order to shed light on the ways in which femininity constitutes a destiny. And this goal structures the organization of the book.

The Second Sex is almost eight hundred pages long, divided in two volumes. The first one, titled *Facts and Myths*, examines, in three parts, the way this situation is built by men. In the first part, titled "Destiny," Beauvoir reviews the way femininity is conceived from the perspective of biology, psychoanalysis, and Marxism. In the second part, "History," Beauvoir proposes a history of women that brings to light the permanence of their oppression by men. Lastly, in the third part, "Myths," Beauvoir studies the way myths and literature in general manifest the way women are constructed by the male gaze. This first, very rich volume shows that the response to the question "What is a woman?" is usually given by men, for men. Men constitute, by their dominance and for their pleasure, women as destined to be their slaves and the objects of their desire.

In the second volume, titled *Lived Experience*, which is almost twice as long as the first volume, Beauvoir inverts the perspective and analyzes the feminine destiny at the different stages of the life of a woman and through the lens of what she calls different figures. In four parts ("Formation," "Situation," "Justifications," and "Toward Liberation"), Beauvoir describes the way in which the male gaze that she described in the first volume shapes the world in such a way that women's experiences can be generalized in typical experiences and figures. She thus proceeds to generalize to an extent that leads her to talk about *the* little girl, *the* young woman, *the* mother. This does not mean that she assumes all girls, all women, and all mothers have the same individual experiences. On the contrary, she shows how these different figures are situations, that is, social positions that are always already interpreted and normed for the women who access them. According to her, "it is thus necessary to study woman's traditional destiny carefully" to understand what the ground on which women's freedom can affirm itself is:

> When I use the word "woman" or "feminine", I obviously refer to no archetype, to no immutable essence; "in the present state of education and customs" must be understood to follow most of my affirmations. There is no question of expressing eternal truths here, but of describing the common ground from which all singular feminine existence stems.[33]

While the whole book focuses on femininity, this femininity is studied from a rejection of the idea of a feminine essence and from an analysis of the economic, social, and political situation of women, not first from their individual one.

To be a woman is therefore to be in a certain economic, social, and political situation. This situation implies a set of norms according to which women are conditioned to behave and on the basis of which they are judged. To be a woman, a "real" woman, implies conforming to these norms. And in the same way one questions the nature of a tool when it stops working, a woman's femininity starts being questioned when a gap appears between her behavior and the behavior that is socially prescribed to her. Yet, what is the behavior prescribed to women in society? Submission.

4

Elusive Submission

Submission, as we have seen, is an ordinary experience lived by everyone and particularly by women. To study it, the usual perspective on power must be turned upside down. Power cannot be considered anymore as being simply unidirectional, originating from a person who wields it to someone upon whom it is exerted. These two dimensions of submission—its mundane character and the inversion of the perspective that its comprehension calls for—make it difficult to know what submission is or how the inferior party in an unequal power relation is affected. These difficulties are further reinforced when one studies the submission of women specifically. So many things have been said and written about female submission by those who have wished for it or (more rarely) by those who have condemned it, but the very situation of submission has made it difficult for these women's experience to be expressed and heard. Yet if we understand, with Beauvoir, that the response to the question "What is a woman?" is probably "A woman is a person who is not born submissive but becomes it," then this silencing should be opposed. Every effort should be made to understand not only how submission is lived but also how it appears to women, to all women, as a preordained destiny.

Submission is hard to describe and even harder to understand. To grasp what it means, two major philosophical problems need to be addressed: first, the problem of knowing how to conceptualize the ordinary, and second, the problem of knowing how to conceptualize power.

Submission and Ordinary Life

Ordinary life defies philosophical analysis. Insofar as it belongs to ordinary behaviors, submission thus poses three problems to philosophy: a theoretical problem, an epistemological problem, and a moral problem.

The theoretical issue that the ordinary raises for philosophy is the problem of its worth: Is the ordinary worthy of philosophical investigation? Do we really have something to say about the mundane abdications, about the moment we submit to our boss, or about the moment we let our husband decide for us? Shouldn't philosophy be more preoccupied with abstract truths, the existence of God, morality, than with the description of our everyday behaviors? The gendered division of labor and the consequences of new managerial techniques on workers' lives can appear to some as trivial matters compared to the "big questions" regarding the nature of being or the possibility of knowing the outside world. If philosophy is to tackle only "big" and noble issues, it is unclear whether submission is one of them. Knowing what is worth philosophical attention is in itself a philosophical question, which has important moral and political repercussions.[1] In the case of submission, this theoretical problem can be addressed in two ways. First, philosophy, from Plato and Aristotle to Heidegger, arises from a form of wonder in the face of the most mundane elements of human existence. The mundane and unthought character of submission should function as an incentive to take up submission as a topic of philosophical inquiry. Second, the fact that submission has not until now been a philosophical subject is not necessarily ascribable to its being a non-philosophical theme or experience. The social status of canonical philosophers, apart from Epictetus the slave, gives us good reason to think that if submission has not been a topic of notable philosophical study, it is probably because these philosophers had such a privileged social situation that the experience of submission was not a part of their everyday lives. Making submission a philosophical subject is only possible in the context of a democratization of philosophy. If philosophy is not exclusively practiced by members of the social elite nor exclusively intended for them, then understanding everyone's ordinary life is a task that falls on philosophy. And in this life, submission is a common and shared experience.

The epistemological and moral problem that the ordinary character of submission raises for philosophy is more troubling: it derives from the link between submission and the mediocrity of the ordinary. In its literal meaning, "mediocre" is used to qualify something as average and, therefore, lacking in interest and attraction. To say that the ordinary is mediocre in that sense is obvious and demonstrates why it is so hard to say anything about it: the ordinary is precisely what we do not think about because nothing distinguishes it, because it has no edge that thought could hold onto in order to grasp it and say something about it. In this respect, the ordinary is a real challenge for philosophy: by its very nature, it seems like there is nothing to say or think about it. Although we might think that what is for us most mundane is also the easiest to know, as soon as we try to take hold of the ordinary, it slips through our fingers. This is the sense of the criticism put forth by Nietzsche, in the nineteenth century, to the upholders of the Platonic idea that knowing something would be recognizing what we already know. He thus writes:

> Even the most cautious among them suppose that what is familiar is at least *more easily knowable* than what is strange, and that, for example, sound method demands that we start from the "inner world," from the "facts of consciousness," because this world is *more familiar to us*. Error of errors! What is familiar is what we are used to; and what we are used to is most difficult to "know"—that is, to see as a problem; that is, to see as strange, as distant, as "outside us."
>
> The great certainty of the natural sciences in comparison with psychology and the critique of the elements of consciousness—one might almost say, with the *unnatural* sciences—is due precisely to the fact that they choose for their object what is *strange*, while it is almost contradictory and absurd to even *try* to choose for an object what is not-strange.[2]

Knowledge requires distancing oneself from its object—this distance is precisely what allows for objectivity—and this distance is contrary to our relation to the ordinary. Nietzsche's text highlights two important ways in which the ordinary is an obstacle to knowledge. On the one hand, knowing what is close to us is difficult precisely because it is close to us. And on the other hand, questioning what is close to us, that is, considering it as a problem that calls for attention and analysis, is not easy. In this respect, the inherent difficulty of analyzing submission is clear: if submission is indeed a very ordinary experience for human beings, then it does not require any specific analysis. We submit, and so what? But even if such an analysis is conducted, it will stumble over the particular difficulty that we have in comprehending our most ordinary experiences.[3]

The mediocre (in the literal sense) character of the ordinary makes understanding it difficult; its mediocrity in a *negative* sense raises a moral issue. "Mediocre" indeed does not only mean "average." What is mediocre, in everyday language, is often what is below average or what is, if not really bad, at least clearly disappointing. The common perception of the ordinary has something to do with this negative understanding of mediocrity. Our thought processes are hindered by the ordinary, in what is average, indiscernible, about it, but also and maybe mostly in what is negative and uncomfortable or shameful about it. This effect is particularly prominent in the case of submission. Even if we manage to extract ourselves from the evidence of the ordinary to raise submission as a problem, the examination of this experience seems a bit shameful. To give an example that may be too obvious, in France, people much prefer focusing on the extraordinary courage of the heroes of the French Resistance than on the ordinary submission of the French masses under German occupation. Even when this submission is addressed, it is first and foremost not to bring its ordinary character to light but what is immoral and scandalous in it. This is one of the most audacious aspects of Beauvoir's depiction of her everyday life during the German occupation in her memoirs—where she insists much more on the ordinary and mundane aspect of submission than on the heroic and extraordinary behavior of the members of the Resistance.[4]

This discomfort and disgust with the mediocre is particularly strong in the case of submission, because it is not only an ordinary behavior but also seen as an immoral one. It is taken as self-evident that any human being should first and above all else seek freedom. Therefore, submission, understood as a relinquishment of freedom, appears as a behavior that is contrary to nature and thus immoral. To focus on submission is to examine these behaviors through which humans, in everyday life, go against one of the fundamental values of human life. Finally, in addition to the unpleasantness of any analysis of the ordinary in its mediocrity, the analysis of submission generates embarrassment because of the gap it manifests between what we think and what we do, between what we take for being good and the norms according to which we act.

Once these problems are brought to light, the lack of philosophical study of submission is easy to understand: its philosophical status is not clearly established; conceiving of our ordinary behaviors as a topic worthy of philosophical investigation is difficult; and submission's immorality reinforces the discomfort among those who try to conceptualize the ordinary not only in its plainness but also in its negativity.

An Analysis of Power from the Bottom Up

Nonetheless, an analysis of submission is crucial in order to *think power*.[5] If we proceed without a concept of submission—if we only study asymmetrical power relations from the perspective of domination—we deprive ourselves of a complete understanding of power relations, especially of asymmetrical power relations, as they are considered from only one point of view. Studying domination as an asymmetrical power relationship requires examining both ends of the relation of domination. From the dominant's side, this means wondering how domination works for the one who exerts it. For instance, one can wonder what it does to the dominant to dominate and propose an analysis of the experience of domination; Julius Caesar's *Commentaries on the Gallic War*, in which he narrates in detail his conquest of Gaul, could be a good model. One can also examine the efficiency of domination in studying strategies, techniques, and methods, as, for instance, Machiavelli does in *The Prince*, which exposes how to obtain and keep power. It is also possible to wonder what dominating is, who dominates at a given point in time, and why some agents are trying to dominate. But the issue that is rarely raised, although it is crucial for the analysis of domination, consists in considering how domination works for those on whom it is exerted.

Studying submission thus proceeds to invert our perspective: instead of analyzing asymmetrical power relations from the simple point of view of those who impose or create them, it requires examining them from the point of view of those on whom they are exerted. Understanding the way domination works for those who exert it does not suffice to account for what happens to those on whom it is exerted. The use of the verb "exert" should not confuse us here: domination is a *relation*, as we saw in the figure in the first chapter, so we can make the minimal assumptions that this relation has an effect on who is dominated and that, contrary to what the verb form could seem to imply, the dominated are not absolutely passive in that process. Against a descending conception of power, which consists in thinking that the nature of power is fully grasped when it is seen as an action of the dominant on the dominated, the analysis of submission invites us to proceed from the bottom up, and to think power as inseparable from its effects and from the actions of those who submit to it.

This inversion of the perspective on power is grounded in the idea—which is Marxist in its origin and has been revisited by feminists—that the standpoint from which we study social reality determines the knowledge we obtain of this social reality. The core hypothesis of such an inversion of perspective is thus that examining power relations from the standpoint of those who are submitted to them not only will grant us an additional, complementary outlook on power relations but enable us to acquire a qualitatively better understanding of the social world. It is not only that we will have *more* information but that the information we will obtain will be *better*, because it won't stem from a strategy of domination. As Marx and contemporary theorists of domination, like anthropologist James C. Scott, show, studying domination exclusively from the dominants' point of view produces an account of domination that serves their interests. According to Scott, many people believe that those who are dominated do not resist domination. And they believe this because they rely on what he calls the "public transcript" of domination, that is, what is publicly said about domination and corresponds to "the *self*-portrait of dominant elites as they would have themselves seen."[6] The reason we can be tempted to believe that domination "works" in the sense that it obtains obedience without resistance is that the descriptions we have of domination come from the dominants themselves. But there are also what he calls "hidden transcripts," that is, what is being said and done "offstage," in particular among the dominated when the dominant is not present. And when one pays attention to the diverse "hidden transcripts," a much more complex picture of the power relations emerges, which, in particular, displays a much greater resistance to domination than what is commonly anticipated. In adopting the perspective not of the dominant but of the people submitted to power, and interrogating their experience, we gain a better understanding of domination.

The History of an Inversion

As we have established, thinking about submission entails challenging the commonly adopted perspective on power. This idea of shifting the perspective on power in order to gain a better understanding of it dates back to Marxism. The way it has been developed, notably in history and in the history of ideas, can help us understand the practical issues it raises and how it can best be used to understand women's submission.

In the 1920s in France, historians Lucien Febvre and Marc Bloch founded the journal *Annales d'histoire économique et sociale* (*Annals of Economic and Social History*), which aimed to promote social and long-term history, against the tendency of historical sciences at the time that focused on political, "evental"[7] history, that is, a history that is first and foremost one of kings, kingdoms, and battles. From this journal and its goal to propose a "total history" in place of the traditional history and its emphasis on politics, war, and diplomacy emerged what would become known as the Annales school. This school of thought continued to structure the historical field even after World War II, particularly the works of Georges Duby and Fernand Braudel. Through their rejection of event-centered history and advocacy of scrutinizing long-term economic and social changes, these historians opened up a new perspective on power. In showing that analyzing the comings and goings of kings and lords was not enough to understand the societies they were ruling or even their power over these societies, the Annales school developed and popularized the idea that understanding power demands understanding how this power was experienced by everyday people. When history is written not from the standpoint of those who rule but with a focus on describing and analyzing what happens in the everyday life of people who experience this power, a better knowledge on the functioning of power is obtained.[8]

This evolution of historiography had significant consequences for the philosophical understanding of power. Indeed, the publication of the first volume of Michel Foucault's *History of Sexuality* in 1976 and his course in the Collège de France titled "Society Must Be Defended,"[9] from the same year, can be seen as a philosophical continuation of the Annales school. In "Society Must Be Defended," Foucault sets himself the task of studying a discourse on power in the modern era, which is not what he calls the "philosophico-juridicial" discourse of sovereignty—the descending power of the king on his subjects—but the counterdiscourse, which he calls "historico-political," which conceives war as the permanent background of social relations, even during times of peace. This is not the discourse of sovereignty, or of a pacified legal order, but a discourse of domination and of never-ending war between dominants and dominated. Foucault proposes a shift from the central power, which is the power of the king, to the plural powers, which are multiple reciprocal relations between members of civil society.

This distinction between sovereignty and domination seeks to give a better understanding of what power is and how it structures society. Society is not organized vertically, by the unidirectional power of a sovereign on the people. It is structured horizontally, by a multiplicity of power relations, which are multidirectional, are sometimes silent, and form a net of relations and conflicts. This idea that power is not organized around a single relationship but by a multiplicity of interpersonal relationships is central to understanding the role of an analysis of submission in the broader context of an analysis of power. Instead of identifying it as what La Boétie calls voluntary servitude—a form of blind obedience of the people to its king or tyrant—thinking of submission as the way interpersonal domination is lived by those on which it is exerted is grounded in a similar intent to analytically reconstitute power relations that are usually silenced and yet structure society. In a certain way, what interests me about the concept of submission is to double down on Foucault's gesture: to focus on domination rather than on sovereignty and, within submission, to focus on those who live it rather than those who exercise it.

What Can We Know about Submission?

The problem that we are facing, however, is that it is very hard to study the experience of submissive people because it is silenced by domination. One of the objectives and mechanisms of domination is to silence oppressed people and to ensure that their experiences and their point of view appear as negligible or, even better, do not appear at all. A good example of this dynamic is colonization: one of the mechanisms of colonization is to ensure that the colonizers' point of view triumphs as representing the only available truth. The silencing in social domination functions in two ways. First, one of the effects of social domination is that the dominated are often deprived of the necessary conditions to be able to express themselves—for instance, access to education or to means of communication. Second, the experiences of the dominated people, even if they are expressed, are discounted as being wrong, untrue, dangerous, or immoral.

Because of this silencing, the history of oppressed people is a history marked by a lack of reliable sources. Even when they do exist, they are fragmentary and are not of the same quality as traditional historical sources. To alleviate this problem, historians and philosophers like Michel Foucault use sources that are not the traditional, commonly accepted, reliable ones. Instead of writing history from royal decrees, laws, and military archives, they diversify the sources of history and try to use administrative history as well as testimonies or other "subjugated knowledges,"[10] to use Foucault's expression, to bring to light power in its mundane, local, infinitesimal dimensions.

Analyzing submission as we understand it, the way that the position of inferiority in an interpersonal relationship is lived, and analyzing women's submission in particular, raises specific issues: to analyze female submission, one needs sources about individuals who have historically been deprived of power, on relationships that belong to the private sphere, which are underdocumented, and on relationships where individual and structural dimensions are intertwined. First, works in women's history indeed show that writing the history of women is writing the history of an absence. Historically women had no power; therefore, it is not their history that is to be found in royal decrees and accounts of battles. In 1818 already, Catherine, the heroine of Jane Austen's *Northanger Abbey*, exclaimed:

> History, real solemn history, I cannot be interested in. . . . I read it a little as a duty, but it tells me nothing that does not either vex or weary me. The quarrels of popes and kings, with wars or pestilences, in every page; the men all so good for nothing, and hardly any women at all.[11]

Until the 1970s, history was a history of men's lives, written by men. Writing women's history was first an unveiling: it needed to make visible what had always been hidden or omitted.

Second, women were not living in the public sphere but in the private one. Yet traditionally, history books describe the public sphere only. In general, the history of private life is made difficult by the lack of sources. There is a double silence that obstructs the analysis of women's experiences: women did not write history—or at least they did not for a very long time—and they were not part of the public sphere, which is the one historians wrote about for a very long time. Women's history, as it emerged in the 1970s following Michelle Perrot's pioneering work,[12] is primarily a history of the private sphere and carries with it the difficulties of such a history. This history of women requires an interest in the mundane (the difficulties of which we already mentioned) and in using sources that are not classical, authorized ones but biographies, autobiographies, and partial sources. Autobiographies are partial and only partially reliable because too often only women who have the means to write and who view their experiences as worthy of being told write about their lives; and there are good reasons to think that their experiences are not representative of those of most women.

Finally—and this is probably the most complex epistemological obstacle—the specificity of the power relations in which women find themselves is that the relationship between men and women is not one of domination of one social class or group over another but *individual* relations of domination, which are particularly underdocumented. Women, insofar as they are, for instance, workers, Black, of lower castes, lesbians, or disabled, can find themselves in relations of social domination of one group over another. But as women they endure a form of domination that has a social component but mostly manifests itself in interpersonal relationships.

The first problem this specificity creates is the following: Foucault and the historians of the Annales school are mostly concerned with political power, the way in which the state power functions, the way individuals resist it, or, on the contrary, the way individuals submit to it. When the power under scrutiny is not political in the strictest sense, however, because it is not the power of a ruler over subjects, it is much more difficult to have documentation about this power: a husband does not produce rulings in order to make his wife obey him, so there are no traces of his orders.

Second, it is likely that social hierarchies influence interpersonal hierarchies and that therefore some human beings experience submission (considerably) more than others because they are victims of social oppression. When one is part of an underprivileged social class or from a racialized group, when one is female, gay, lesbian, or trans—that is, when one is in a situation of social inferiority—one is more likely to find oneself as the inferior party in interpersonal hierarchical relations.[13] In patriarchal societies, that is, in societies structured by the domination of women by men, the experience women have of submission when they submit to men is both an individual one—it is a submission of one individual to another—and a structural one insofar as it is prescribed by the structure of society. To understand it, it is thus necessary to utilize sources that document a situation that is structurally silenced.

Can the Subaltern Speak?

However, documenting the situation and experiences of people whose voice is structurally silenced by oppression raises epistemological issues: there is a serious risk of betraying their experiences in imposing on them frameworks of analysis that are foreign to them or of essentializing their experiences. In the case of submission, there is a risk of imposing an understanding of submission that contains a moral condemnation and of thinking women submit because it is in their nature, and thus missing the fact that submitting can be a pragmatic decision.

The problem of documenting or analyzing experiences that are structurally silenced has been brought to light by subaltern studies initially developed by Indian and South Asian academics who were specialists in postcolonial studies. Using the term "subaltern" coined by the Marxist Italian thinker Antonio Gramsci in his theory of cultural hegemony, they endeavor to study people who are subordinated in South Asian societies on the basis of their class, caste, age, or gender. In this context, Gayatri Spivak, an Indian literary critic, wrote a now famous essay titled "Can the Subaltern Speak?"[14] The starting point of Spivak's essay is a 1972 conversation between Michel Foucault and Gilles Deleuze, published under the title "Intellectuals and Power."[15] This conversation focuses on the attitude of the intellectual in the context of questioning the omnipotence of the subject. According to Deleuze, the critique of representation as it has been undertaken by Foucault and the highlighting of the link between knowledge and power are the first steps of a revolution in the thinking about power. And it leads to "the indignity of speaking for others" and in particular, in this context, the impossibility for the intellectual to speak for the proletarians: "theory demanded that only those directly concerned can speak in a practical way on their own behalf."[16]

Gayatri Spivak begins, in her famously obscure style, by attacking this position of Deleuze and Foucault on the grounds that they "systematically ignore the question of ideology and their own implication in intellectual and economic history."[17] According to her, the two philosophers did not get the measure of their contradictions: they ignored the international division of labor, for instance, when they talked about "the workers' struggle" in the singular; their valorization of the oppressed demonstrates an essentialization of the *worker* that is exactly the kind of essentialization they rose up against when discussing non-oppressed subjects. Indeed, she thinks Deleuze and Foucault, in their ivory tower, proposed a certain conception of the experience of the oppressed as transparent and conscious, whereas the experience of the non-oppressed is always studied in what is ideological about it. In proposing to limit themselves to listening to the oppressed, they assumed the oppressed are subjects that are constructed in a non-ideological manner.

This leads Spivak to wonder whether subaltern women[18] can speak and whether feminists can listen to them. What is at stake here is shedding light on a tension between the necessity of taking into account the consciousness of the subaltern woman in academic work, especially in feminist academic work, and the fact that doing so necessarily attributes a subjectivity to this subaltern woman. This attribution of a subjectivity, which is similar to what Spivak perceives in Deleuze and Foucault, is conceived as an epistemic violence in itself because it imposes a particular Western structure to the consciousness of the subaltern woman, a structure that is not hers. Therefore, any attempt to talk about the subaltern woman and to make her speak implies a betrayal of what she is through the imposition of a subjectivity, conceived in a Western way:

> In so fraught a field, it is not easy to ask the question of the consciousness of the subaltern woman. . . . Though all feminist or antisexist projects cannot be reduced to this one, to ignore it is an unacknowledged political gesture that has a long history and collaborates with a masculine radicalism that renders the place of the investigator transparent. In seeking to learn to speak to (rather than listen to or speak for) the historically muted subject of the subaltern woman, the postcolonial intellectual systematically "unlearns" female privilege.[19]

There is thus a conflict from the point of view of the researcher between the desire to advance knowledge and this epistemic violence that hinders it. According to Spivak, overlooking this epistemic violence and this betrayal is as harmful as the hypothesis that researchers could have adopted a transcendental position—that they could be overhanging the people they study.

Spivak's analysis matters for the purposes of this book in several respects. To begin with, it demonstrates the difficulty of any work on submission insofar as it is a work on the lived experience of people who traditionally do not get to speak. As we noted earlier, any work that focuses on the oppressed and the subaltern—people on whom a form of domination is exerted—is confronted with a problem of sources in the broad sense. The very structure of domination implies that dominated people are, at least to a certain extent, deprived of access to speak. This deprivation can be the result of direct obstacles (e.g., not having access to education or to means of expression), but it can also be indirect and result from the fact that such people's voices are made inaudible by the very conditions of discourse.

Even more interesting, however, is that Spivak's analysis shows that it is never possible to transmit or render the subaltern's experience in academic work without betraying it by its very transmission. The same problem appears in a work on submission: there is, first, a risk of essentializing the person whose experience is described. To say about a woman's experience that it is one of submission is to risk implicitly making this woman's submission a part of her essence. The second aspect of the same problem is an even deeper issue, that is, the necessary betrayal of the experience of submission when it is transmitted in a work that aims to be an emancipatory one. It seems that the only solution to this constant problem is to be found in Spivak's claim that "the postcolonial intellectual systematically 'unlearns' female privilege." One must endeavor to systematically unlearn one's privilege—without, out of privilege, presuming that submission is the problem of the women one studies and not also one's own.

Women's submission is thus very hard to study philosophically. Insofar as it refers to a mundane experience, it constantly eludes analysis. Insofar as it necessitates an inversion of perspective on power, it seems impossible because on the one hand it can only be done by the oppressed, and on the other hand it is out of reach for the oppressed since oppression consists precisely in preventing them from talking about and analyzing their experiences.

5

The Experience of Submission

In the face of these apparently insoluble problems in an analysis of submission, it could be tempting to give up on a philosophical analysis of submission once and for all: the epistemological, moral, and political problems posed by submission seem discouraging. Yet, in the same way that her analyses of gender difference have allowed us to overcome the essentialist and constructionist pitfalls and to identify the relationship between womanhood and submission, Beauvoir's original phenomenology provides us with a method that responds to the pitfalls analyzed in the previous chapter and reveals a way to understand and describe what submission is. Because of her privileged social position, she has access to the experience of submission without being silenced like many submissive women are. This position, and the original phenomenological method that she builds, allows her to respond to the conundrum of a bottom-up approach of a dominated phenomenon and to show that the way submission is experienced by women is as a destiny.

A Privileged Position

As we have seen, one major obstacle to describing the experiences of dominated people—and therefore women's experience of submission—is their being silenced. Beauvoir's singular social position, at the intersection of her life as a woman and her education and career as a writer, grants her an exceptional perspective that can remedy this issue. Beauvoir argues that she is in a very particular position that allows her to unveil submission and, more generally, women's experience as it has never been seen.[1] Beauvoir is a woman, and this quality is the first one that comes to her mind when she seeks to define herself (recall that she conceives of *The Second Sex* as a necessary theoretical step to be able to write her memoirs). But it is not only because she is a woman that she can make the feminine condition appear vividly in her work. If men and women are both judge and jury, "certain women are still best suited to elucidate the situation of women." She considers that certain women, among whom she places herself, are in a singular situation: they are women and, at the same time, they "have never felt [their] femaleness to be a difficulty or an obstacle." This is true of them to such an extent that on the one hand they "grasp more immediately what the fact of being female means for a human being," and on the other hand they are able to have a form of detachment and distance when they consider this issue that other women cannot have and that, according to Beauvoir, makes it possible "to hope [their] attitude will be objective," such that they can "afford the luxury of impartiality."[2] Beauvoir insists on this privileged situation in her memoirs:

> No; far from suffering from my femininity, I have, on the contrary, from the age of twenty on, accumulated the advantages of both sexes; after *She Came to Stay*, those around me treated me both as a writer, their peer in the masculine world, and as a woman; this was particularly noticeable in America: at the parties I went to, the wives all got together and talked to each other while I talked to the men, who nevertheless behaved toward me with greater courtesy than they did toward the members of their own sex. I was encouraged to write *The Second Sex* precisely because of this privileged position. It allowed me to express myself in all serenity.[3]

We can of course have some doubts about the fact that Beauvoir was always treated by her companions as an equal and, even more, about the idea that she never experienced femininity as an obstacle, which is contradicted by many passages from her *Memoirs of a Dutiful Daughter*. The way she responds to the standpoint issue is nonetheless interesting: because she is a woman, she grew up in a world made for girls and women, she has firsthand experience of what being a woman is like, and she has had direct access to diverse feminine experiences. Then her education, her life as an intellectual woman, and her situation as a writer opened up possibilities for her that were generally not available to women.

As Beauvoir says when she explains why women have such difficulty being creative geniuses, creation is an "attempt . . . to found the world anew on a human freedom: that of the creator; to foster such an ambition, one must first unequivocally posit oneself as a freedom."[4] One needs considerable confidence in the legitimacy of one's place in the world in order to have the ambition—or pretention even—necessary to creation. Beauvoir is in a singular situation in that regard: her education and her personal qualities have enabled her to acquire such a pretention that is usually out of reach for women. Traditionally, because of male domination, women have not had the opportunity or even the desire to leave a written trace of their experience, since their experience is already deemed negligible. Beauvoir would have faced the same obstacles, but because of her father's financial problems, among other things, she was allowed to study like a man and to excel like a man—to the extent that she is, at the same time, a woman in her experiences and a man in the understanding she has of the importance of her existence.

It is thus clear that Beauvoir finds herself at the improbable intersection of an oppressed social situation, which grants her access to a certain truth of the social reality that is usually hidden, and of a social privilege that enables her to think, to write, and to be read and heard. This double position allows her to not be silenced like Spivak's subalterns, to be able to express a worldview, and, at the same time, to make salient certain aspects of life that male philosophers cannot see or do not want to see.

Indeed, as we saw, philosophy struggles to grasp ordinary life not only because it seems too mediocre for philosophers to take interest in but also because they are, by their social position, shielded from this ordinary. For instance, feminist epistemology, which studies, among other matters, the way in which women and men have access to different knowledge, shows the following: in the same way that mechanics are better than non-mechanics at seeing the mechanical issues of an engine in front of them, women *see* certain things that men do not because of the gendered division of labor. Because women are appointed to cleaning and tidying up, they see, for instance, dirty socks on the floor that men do not even notice. It does not come from the fact that women are naturally more able to perceive dirty laundry or that men are blind to housework but from the fact that perception has a social dimension and is shaped by the gendered division of labor: women perceive dirty socks more because they are the ones in charge of doing laundry.

As a woman and insofar as women traditionally oversee domestic life, Beauvoir manages to bring to light ordinary life in all of its complexity, from the philosophical issues brought about by housework and cooking to the stakes of menstruation and puberty in one's bodily experience. Lastly and more specifically, this position allows Beauvoir to grasp female submission in a particularly acute way: as a woman, she distinguishes in herself, and in the women around her, the pleasures of devotion, and of abdication. As an existentialist intellectual for whom freedom is the cardinal value, she is scandalized by the spectacle of women's submission. This tension between the temptation of submission, which she identifies in herself in *Memoirs of a Dutiful Daughter*, for instance, and the reflex of rejection and condemnation of submission, which appears repeatedly when she describes the housewife in *The Second Sex*, is precisely what allows her to shed light on submission in its complexity and to call for its analysis.

An Original Phenomenological Method

We have also seen that studying submission requires an inversion of the perspective in order to examine power from the bottom up and that such an inversion stumbles on complex epistemological issues. Beauvoir's position allows her to see and to make seen women's experience, and their experience of submission in particular, in a resolutely novel way, but she also proposes an appropriate method to solve the problems that the ordinary and a bottom-up analysis of power raise. In order to do this, Beauvoir takes inspiration from phenomenology,[5] which is a philosophical school of thought as well as a philosophical method. Phenomenology as a discipline appeared with the German philosopher Edmund Husserl at the end of the nineteenth century (though other philosophers used this term before him) and developed in numerous directions during the twentieth century.

THE HERITAGE OF THE APRICOT COCKTAIL

When Husserl created phenomenology, his ambition was to propose a science of subjective experience through which philosophy would "go back to the things themselves." To do so, Husserl was interested in the way consciousness is lived, that is, consciousness in the first person. For instance, what was at stake was describing and analyzing what seeing, hearing, and feeling, but also walking and talking, are for the subject who lives these experiences. Beauvoir recounts in her memoirs the first time that she and Sartre heard about Husserl: Raymond Aron, a young philosopher and good friend of Sartre at the time, who was returning from a stay in Berlin during which he had discovered Husserl, pointed out the apricot cocktail that was in front of him and said, "You see, my dear fellow, if you are a phenomenologist, you can talk about this cocktail and that's philosophy!" This episode convinced Sartre that phenomenology was the method that would enable him to "talk about things just as he saw and touched them, and that it would be philosophy." For him as for Beauvoir, it became possible to "affirm . . . simultaneously both the sovereignty of conscience and the presence of the world."[6]

Beyond the anecdote, Beauvoir retains several things from Husserl: first, that phenomenology studies lived experiences and shows that they allow us to access something about the meaning of the world. Beauvoir adopts this idea when she chooses to use the concept of "lived experience" in the title of the second volume of *The Second Sex*, which is the direct translation of the Husserlian concept of *Erlebnis*. The message is clear: what is at stake for her is to study the lived experiences of women in order to access the meaning of the reality "woman" in the world. From the multiple experiences that she compiles and analyzes, Beauvoir makes it possible to provide a picture of what a woman is, not from the perspective of men—which is usually the only considered perspective—but from the perspectives and the experiences of women.

The second lesson Beauvoir retains from Husserl, which is inseparable from the focus on lived experience, is the central place of the first person. Phenomenology in every shape and form is interested in consciousness and experience insofar as they are experiences in the first person—experiences made by a subject and analyzed from the point of view of this subject.

One of the central ideas of phenomenology is that every act of consciousness is an intentional one, an act directed toward the world. In the context of a reflection on what being a woman can mean, resorting to the first person has a particular significance. As Beauvoir shows in the first volume of *The Second Sex*, the transformation, by men, of women into the Other comes in part from the way men appropriated objectivity and the third person for themselves. Adopting the first person is thus a strong and feminist act in itself.

Last, it is thanks to Husserl and his heirs that Beauvoir manages to bring out one of the important elements of any philosophy of the ordinary: the role of the body. Husserl, in *Ideen II*, starts from the fact that there are two ways to experience material bodies: as mere physical things or as living bodies. While science considers material bodies as simple physical things—in physics, for instance, when wondering at what speed a body moves in a space, scientists measure this speed and establish theories and laws—the natural attitude conceives the body as alive, which is a conception that is radically different from the scientific one. According to Husserl, the living body is different from the physical body in four ways: (1) the living body appears as a field of feelings; (2) it is the departure point of all spontaneous movement; (3) it functions as the fixed point of our orientation in space; and (4) it takes part in causal relations. In later works, Husserl provides a list of phenomenological issues to be studied: he mentions the problem of death and birth, the problem of the unconscious, the problem of historicity and social life, and, finally, what he calls "the problem of the sexes."[7] In the role she grants to the lived body in her analysis (and to which we will soon return), Beauvoir clearly inscribes herself in the methodological and thematical descent of the late Husserl and his heirs, the first of whom was Maurice Merleau-Ponty.[8]

THE ORIGINALITY OF THE BEAUVOIRIAN METHOD

From this heritage, Beauvoir devises in *The Second Sex* a phenomenological method that consists in granting a crucial role to the description of multiple first persons. At the end of the introduction, she sets herself the task of "describ[ing] the world from the woman's point of view such as it is offered to her."[9] While the first volume, devoted to the way woman has been constituted as the Other by men, allows us to understand how submission comes to appear as a destiny for women, the second volume describes this submission from the women's point of view. In this respect, *The Second Sex* is a source of inestimable importance for those interested in women's situation and in their possible consent to this submission, as the book is the first phenomenological analysis of women's submission.

Beauvoir's analysis erases once and for all the suspicion of a paternalistic, overhanging, imperialist approach to submission: with her work, it appears clear that submission is not an attitude of "other" women who would manifest their lack of desire for freedom by wearing a veil or by their resignation to their situation. To the contrary, in proposing a phenomenology of the lived experience of submission by all women, in all ages, in all situations, Beauvoir reveals the generalized and almost universal character of female submission. Almost all women are submissive to a certain extent. This characteristic does not derive from women's universal taste for submission but from the fact—established in the first volume—that the world in which female human beings are born is always already structured by a norm of femininity, that is, a norm of submission.

The second volume of *The Second Sex* is surprising for seasoned readers of philosophy: for over four hundred pages, Beauvoir compiles personal experience, excerpts from literary and scientific works, and testimonies, in an abundance of facts and details, in order to propose a description of "woman's traditional destiny":

> How woman is taught to assume her condition, how she experiences this, what universe she finds herself enclosed in, and what escape mechanisms are permitted to her, here's what I will seek to describe.[10]

The description of women's condition is conceived by Beauvoir as the necessary prerequisite of any conception of women's emancipation.[11]

This description is deeply original on three levels. First, it describes women's lives, in their complexity and diversity, which had not been done in philosophy until then. Second, it is original because it does not describe their lives from an external point of view but their lives *as they live them*. In general, and as the first volume shows, women's lives are analyzed or discussed only from the perspective of men. Women are always objects—objects of study and sexual objects. In *The Second Sex*, for the first time, women appear as a multiplicity of subjects. To accomplish this, Beauvoir is a phenomenologist insofar as she relies on first-person experiences, but she is an original phenomenologist because she multiplies the sources of first-person narratives.

This characteristic is inseparable from the third level of originality, which is to be found in the position of Beauvoir herself. Unlike Sartre and other phenomenologists, Beauvoir does not use the first person to describe women's lived experience and thus clearly signifies that what is in question in not her personal, individual experience. When *The Second Sex* was released in France, Beauvoir became the target of sexist attacks. The novelist François Mauriac wrote to Roger Stéphane, an employee of *Les Temps modernes*, Beauvoir and Sartre's journal, "Your employer's vagina has no secrets from me,"[12] as if the book had been unveiling Beauvoir's sexuality. On the contrary, *The Second Sex* is not autobiographical. Beauvoir uses the third person to describe women's experiences, and the severity with which she sometimes judges them indicates that these descriptions are not autobiographical. They come from meticulous research on a multiplicity of diaries, memoirs of famous women, and studies in psychology and sociology. At the same time, unlike sociologists and social scientists—who often are, or think they are, in a position of exteriority with what they describe—it is very clear (and she claims it) that Beauvoir is judge and jury. When she describes the everyday life of the housewife or the experience of motherhood, she does not describe her own experiences. Her personal experience, however, is one of the sources on which she grounds her descriptions. This is clear, for instance, when one compares the developments on the young girl's dreams about prince charming in *The Second Sex* with the way in which Beauvoir narrates her own fantasies about love as a teenager in *Memoirs of a Dutiful Daughter*.

Beauvoir's analyses are neither simple generalizations from individual experience—which is often the case in Sartrean phenomenology—nor scientific, objective, remote analyses of other people's experiences. Beauvoir uses her own personal experiences, the experiences of her friends, and her observations of everyday life,[13] as well as literary and scientific works, to generalize from a multiplicity of lives and of first-person experiences and reveal typical experiences and typical figures. Her work, then, does not display the shortcomings of a subjectivist and particular analysis nor of the masculine analysis that freezes the diversity of experiences in the assumption of a feminine essence. Against an "eternal feminine" that means to be universalizing, fixed, and ahistorical, Beauvoir brings to light singular experiences that, when placed side by side, are not particular cases but singular declinations of the first-person experience of what a woman is. This multiplication of points of view is important, particularly because it allows her to erase the specificities of this or that individual, and this or that situation, to bring out a more general experience. Phenomenology's function, for Beauvoir, is not—as is the case, albeit differently, for Husserl, Heidegger, and Sartre—to propose a philosophy of knowledge or of the world itself. It is put in the service of an analysis of a specific situation—women's—that cannot be accessed except by the description of first-person experiences.

Beauvoir holds together phenomenology and a Marxist approach to the social world and thus develops a method of her own that enables her to show how women's situation is lived by them. She borrows from Heidegger the idea that the situation of individuals always already has a meaning, over which they only have partial control. And she refuses to constrain herself to the strict point of view of the individual[14] since she uses multiple sources providing multiple points of view. In proposing different lived experiences of the same situation, she emphasizes how this situation is a given, a destiny, in the face of which women need to take a stand. And in paying attention to the influence of the legal and economic[15] structures on women's situation, she takes seriously the Marxist idea of a need for an analysis of the infrastructure and the superstructure in order to understand interpersonal relationships, without at the same time renouncing the existential dimension of these relations.[16] In this second volume, Beauvoir thus proposes a phenomenology of her own, which results from her appropriation of different components of existential phenomenology and which allows her to solve methodological problems inherent to an analysis of women's submission.

Phenomenology and the Silence of the Oppressed

The phenomenological method enables Beauvoir to propose an analysis of women's submission that would not reproduce the masculine gesture of objectification and that would respond at least partly to the problem raised by the silencing of the oppressed. On the one hand, the phenomenological method itself allows her to adopt a perspective that is not top-down but rather bottom-up on agents' experiences. On the other hand, it allows her to bring out regularities and, implicitly, to show women that their personal experience—which they perceive to be idiosyncratic—is in reality largely shared. That is to say, that the personal is political.

THE SILENCE OF THE OPPRESSED

As we noted earlier, studying submission consists in analyzing the relationship of domination from the point of view of those who live it from a position of inferiority. It thus involves in part wondering how this position of inferiority is lived and analyzed. But we also saw that providing a bottom-up approach of the experience of oppressed people—which is in many ways silenced—is a methodological conundrum.[17]

Beauvoir's adoption of a phenomenological method gives her a way out of this conundrum.[18] As the contemporary uses of phenomenology in social sciences demonstrate, phenomenology inverts the usual movement of the analysis. Where the researcher usually looks for objective regularities among individuals, and where they are wary of any trace of subjectivity that would obscure the neutrality of their perspective, phenomenologists work in the reverse way: they start from their personal experience or from the subjective experiences of other individuals and, from these inner experiences, they proceed to an analysis understood as a movement of exteriorization. As Bruno Frère and Sébastien Laoureux show in the book they devoted to the use of phenomenology in social sciences, this use

> responds in many fields of social sciences to the desire to break off with overhanging approaches of the world, of the space, of subjects. Below the general structures that shape life . . . , researchers seek to grasp what makes sense here and now, before postulating the existence of general frameworks that would need to be uncovered. The singular

carries the universal in itself but in order to show it, one must plunge in the human lives that are made of immediate relations to the body, to animals, to things, and to others. Phenomenology seems to be the most relevant perspective to dissect in their subtlety the matter of these lives and what in them can be generalized.[19]

In this way, in reproducing numerous accounts that she extracted from personal interviews, memoirs, and literary and scientific texts, Beauvoir manages to bring out, to a certain extent, the voices of submissive women who are usually silenced.

SOCIAL STRUCTURE

Beauvoir uses phenomenology in an original manner: she recognizes its ability to reveal individual experiences, but it also allows her to show how the "great structures that shape life" function and how they are lived by individuals. Beauvoir thus holds together the individual and the structure in a constant back-and-forth: in the second volume, phenomenology is used to explore the traditional destiny of women, which is the way social norms and male domination structure them as individuals.

Phenomenology is used at the service both of an ascending inductive process—understanding the general situation of women from particular cases—and a descending process—understanding the way in which the general situation of women influences lived experiences of particular women. As we saw earlier, the first volume, *Facts and Myths*, responds to the question "What is a woman?" from the usual (male) point of view, the one that considers woman as the Other. The second volume, *Lived Experience*, opens with a complete change of perspective and standpoint, since Beauvoir uses phenomenology to analyze what being a woman *does* to women. The adoption of these two standpoints is justified by the idea that the essence question "What is a woman?" cannot be given an abstract response, one that would be given outside the society in which it is raised. It is impossible to conceive of a transcendental subject situated outside the gender difference and able to analyze it objectively. In the context of male domination in which Beauvoir writes and situates herself, what woman is is what she is for men and what this male conception does to her. Beauvoir thus explains this duality of standpoints in the introduction:

> So we will begin by discussing woman from a biological, psychoanalytical, and historical materialist point of view. We will then attempt to positively demonstrate how "feminine reality" has been constituted, why woman has been defined as Other, and what the consequences have been from men's point of view. Then we will describe the world from the woman's point of view such as it is offered to her, and we will be able to understand the difficulties women are up against just when, trying to escape the sphere they have been assigned until now, they have the ambition to be part of the human Mitsein.[20]

Phenomenology, in the second volume, highlights two different phenomena: the (descending) way in which the male point of view structures women's lived experience and, through induction, the reality of the experience of submission; what submission is and how this submission inscribes itself in bodies, in thoughts, in feelings, in the lived experiences of women—in short, from the external structuring of their situation of absolute Other by men.

This point is probably one of the most complex as well as most interesting ones of the Beauvoirian appropriation of phenomenology. She goes beyond the description of women's condition and of their lived experiences as a sociologist might. The woman that is described is not a sort of generalization of the particular women that are in that situation. What is described in each chapter is in a way the Heideggerian "one" of each of these situations, which means the way in which—according to the social norms in effect at this time—women should behave and the way they should experience their situation. To be sure, what she describes also corresponds to the way in which women behave on average, but it is precisely because any social norm, if it functions as a norm in the prescriptive sense, ends up describing what is statistically average. In the Beauvoirian perspective, however, it is very important to keep in mind the fact that the described experiences are those that are imposed on women and not the ones women live, even though, in practice, these experiences overlap or are identical. The fact that Beauvoir clearly conceives the first three parts of the second volume as the description of a destiny that is imposed on women and in which they are always already thrown justifies, in Beauvoir's eyes, that she casts judgment on them:

As housework is an exhausting maintenance of the status quo, the husband—when he comes home—notices disorder and negligence but takes order and neatness for granted. He attaches more positive importance to a well-prepared meal. The triumphant moment of the cook is when she places a successful dish on the table: husband and children welcome it warmly, not only with words, but also by consuming it joyously. . . . It is only in the guests' mouths that the cook's work finds its truth; she needs their votes; she demands that they appreciate her dishes, that they take more; she is irritated if they are no longer hungry: to the point that one does not know if the fried potatoes are destined for the husband or the husband for the fried potatoes. This ambivalence is found in the housewife's whole attitude.[21]

In this description, the housewife seems a bit ridiculous; she has overinflated expectations, she reacts disproportionately, and the ambivalence of her behavior seems to amuse Beauvoir. It is only when the specificity of her use of phenomenology is understood that the fact that Beauvoir's tendency to judge these women takes its real meaning. To be sure, Beauvoir adopts a position of exteriority, but this position is not one of superiority. Beauvoir does not judge real women who would be lying to themselves; she severely judges the female behavior that is prescribed by the way men structure women's destinies.

SUBMISSION IS A DESTINY

In that regard, the phenomenological method renders visible a crucial point, both for Beauvoir's analysis and for our inquiry: through her analysis of women's traditional destiny, Beauvoir shows that women, at every age, in every situation, are destined to submit to men. This means that from the way they are raised and educated, to the way social norms function, submission appears as the behavior that is prescribed to them and that is valorized for them. Beauvoir describes the ways in which boys are encouraged to climb, run, and fight, even at the risk of hurting themselves; girls, on the other hand, are encouraged to be calm and obedient and to accept that they are not allowed to do lots of the things boys can do because such behavior would be dangerous and, more importantly, unfit for them. When boys are encouraged to be adventurous, girls are presented with passivity and submission as ideal behaviors.

This destiny does not appear to be a source of joy. In the wonderfully rich pages Beauvoir devotes to describing in detail the experience of housework, she notes how little girls resist this destiny of a homemaker whose function consists, every day, in fighting untidiness and dirt:

> Few tasks are more similar to the torment of Sisyphus than those of the housewife; day after day, one must wash dishes, dust furniture, mend clothes that will be dirty, dusty, and torn again. . . . I recall an essay of a sixteen-year-old student that opened with words like these: "Today is housecleaning day. I hear the noise of the vacuum Mama walks through the living room. I would like to run away. I swear when I grow up, there will never be a housecleaning day in my house." The child thinks of the future as an indefinite ascent toward some unidentified summit. Suddenly in the kitchen, where her mother is washing dishes, the little girl realizes that over the years, every afternoon at the same time, these hands have plunged into greasy water and wiped the china with a rough dish towel. And until death they will be subjected to these rites. Eat, sleep, clean . . . the years no longer reach

toward the sky, they spread out identical and gray as a horizontal tablecloth; every day looks like the previous one; the present is eternal, useless, and hopeless.[22]

Girls see clearly how they are destined to these repetitive and unpleasant tasks, which are necessary for men to be able to lead an adventurous life and which contradict their own adventurous impulses.

Beauvoir thus escapes the apparently unanswerable question of knowing which kind of epistemic exteriority would enable us to know who is submissive and who is not, and who is authentic and who is not. On the contrary, she sheds light—through an abundance of details, facts, and interwoven experiences—on the following evidence: the common feature of all the female figures she studies, chapter after chapter, is the ambiguity of women's existence and the permanent contradiction between the freedom they have as human beings and the way male domination reduces them to the status of object and absolute Other. In the face of this contradiction experienced by all women, submission is the attitude that is prescribed by the situation in which women find themselves. In that regard, submission does not appear as an exceptional phenomenon, as a deviation from the norm, but, on the contrary, as the attitude prescribed by the "one," that is, by the social norm. What "one" does when one is a woman is to submit.

The Experience of All Women?

In the face of this phenomenological method, however, a suspicion arises: Are the generalizations proposed by Beauvoir as valid as she suggests? When she talks about "woman," is she really talking about all women, no matter where they live, their social class, or their race? The history of feminism is often represented through the metaphor of "waves": after the first wave of feminism, at the end of the nineteenth and beginning of the twentieth century, in which the central struggle was the right to vote, came a second wave, to which *The Second Sex* gave birth, which was concerned with gender equality and in particular women's rights to not be confined to the private sphere. But this second wave has been strongly criticized by some feminists—who are seen as constituting a third wave—who attack the second wave for its blindness to the diversity of women's situations. According to these third wave feminists, many feminists who precede them and are predominantly white Western women from privileged or at least middle-class backgrounds have a tendency to view all women as having a common experience qua women, although this supposedly female experience is actually limited to white Western privileged women. By contrast, third wave feminists argue that an intersectional[23] approach is necessary, one that takes into account the diversity of oppressions, based on race, class, gender, and sexuality, and the way these oppressions intersect with each other such that Black women, for instance, are not just oppressed qua women or qua Black but suffer from a specific oppression qua Black women that is not a mere addition of the two.

In this respect, Beauvoir has been attacked several times on the generalizations she makes in the phenomenological part of *The Second Sex*. For instance, British anthropologist Judith Okely accused Beauvoir of providing an anthropological study of the women in the village of Saint-Germain des Prés—the wealthy Parisian neighborhood where Sartre and Beauvoir were living—in which Beauvoir would implicitly, and (according to Okely) unfairly, set herself as a paradigmatic case rather than a study on women's experiences.[24] Beauvoir is unaware of the very idea of intersectionality (the concept as such did not exist at the time, but she could have paid attention to the possible intersections of oppression, especially since her extensive reading on racial issues partly gave birth to her idea of *The Second Sex*). It is also true that Beauvoir seems to systematically make reductive assumptions about women: she distinguishes so clearly the experience of the woman and the experience of the Black individual that she does not seem to consider the experience of Black women; she also considers that working outside of the house is a way for women to be free, without seeing that in lower social classes, especially among non-white women, most women work outside the house out of necessity, not liberation;[25] and the only non-Western women she refers to are women who live in harems, about whom she reproduces an orientalist and cliché vision.

Despite these indisputable weaknesses, for the past seventy years *The Second Sex* has provided women from around the world a description of womanhood with which they could identify.[26] After publishing the book, Beauvoir received letters from readers from all over the world and from women of various social backgrounds. Despite their diversity, these letters all say more or less the same thing: reading *The Second Sex* was for these female readers the end of a solitude. It enabled them to understand their existence and their femininity. The thousands of letters Beauvoir received (as well as the geographical diversity of their writers) are important in grasping the success of her phenomenological analysis. Even if women do not have the exact same experience of what it is to be a woman,

Beauvoir's readers have found in her book descriptions that have resonated with their own experiences. In reading Beauvoir, some women see, for instance, that the discomfort they have felt in seeing themselves scrutinized in their new female bodies during puberty was a largely shared experience, or that the frustration they experienced when they were seeing their family quickly consume meals they had spent hours preparing was common for many other women. Because Beauvoir systematically situates these experiences as the product of the domination of women by men, she enables readers to experience this central thesis of feminism: the personal is political. Female readers become conscious of the fact that their individual and singular experience has so many common features with the experience of the other women described by Beauvoir; it cannot be considered as a sheer singular experience. Instead, it is the result of a common situation of oppression. It is not because their husbands are particularly bad or their children particularly ungrateful that their existence is the way it is but because they are women and, in this respect, are destined to submission, although as human beings they aspire to freedom.

In short, while submission seemed to resist philosophical analysis, Beauvoir establishes a method that renders this difficult philosophy of the everyday experience of oppressed people possible. In so doing, she modifies what philosophy is:[27] she speaks in the first person and uses other first-person experiences, including those of prostitutes, of anonymous women, voices that philosophy had never imagined listening to until then. She describes subjects that were viewed as non-philosophical because of their ordinary character, from housework to menstruation to female desire. She thus uses her privileged position of a female writer to show that philosophy had not taken seriously what occupies and preoccupies women, particularly their submission. This partly answers the question of why so little had been said about submission in the philosophical discourse: submission emerges as a subject of analysis when philosophy becomes accessible to people like Beauvoir who experienced it and who are interested in using the tools of philosophy to study oppression.

6

Submission Is an Alienation

Thus far, we have established that submission is a very mundane experience for women and that it is socially prescribed to them to the extent that it is experienced by them as a destiny. However, we have not yet understood why women can seem to accept this submission nor why this submission is problematic. This chapter will show that women's submission is the manifestation of the oppression created by patriarchy. More precisely, we will see that submission is the result of women's alienation, which occurs through their objectification, especially their sexual objectification.

In order to do so, we will see how the combination of Beauvoir's theory of situation and her phenomenological method enables her (and us) to understand the mechanism through which women end up submitting: the oppression of women by men happens through a process of alienation—of transformation into an Other—which consists in an objectification of women.

Women are taught throughout their lives that they are objects for men—who see women as radically other than themselves—and this objectification works so well that women see themselves as the Other and not primarily as subjects. Women submit to men because they are always already considered to be objects and not subjects by men and (therefore) by themselves.

Oppression as Alienation

To understand how women's condition is specifically marked by submission, Beauvoir uses the Hegelian theory of domination as alienation and contrasts femininity and other determinations stemming from oppressions in order to establish the specificity of women's oppression. She compares the woman to the Black, the Jew, and the proletarian, other figures constituted by a situation of oppression.[1] This comparison, as we saw, is problematic insofar as it implicitly denies the possibility of multiple identities (these other figures seem to imply that the woman would necessarily be white, Christian, and bourgeois).[2] Yet, it still functions in a way that highlights what these different forms of oppression have in common—oppression consists, from the oppressors' side, in constructing the oppressed as others—and what is specific about women's oppression—the absolute character of women's otherness.

OPPRESSION, OR THE OPPRESSED TRANSFORMED INTO AN OTHER

In order to understand Beauvoir's account of women's oppression, one must first understand Hegel's account of domination, against which Beauvoir builds her own account. For Beauvoir, as for many philosophers and progressives in the twentieth century, one of the best explanatory models of oppression is to be found in the famous and often obscure "master-slave dialectic." This expression refers to Hegel's analysis of interpersonal relationships in the *Phenomenology of Spirit* (though he does not use this expression himself). This analysis is grounded on an anthropological hypothesis (about what humans are and do) and a historical one, and it has been read as a narrative of social emancipation.

Hegel's main anthropological hypothesis is that our relationship with the other is primarily a conflictual one. For Hegel, one of the main differences between humans and animals is the fact that humans can have what he calls self-consciousness: this means not only that consciousness of objects implies an awareness of self, as a subject, but also that being a subject is being aware that we are objects for the other people we encounter, just as they are objects for us. In Section B of the *Phenomenology of Spirit*, Hegel explains that in order to access self-consciousness, humans need recognition. Therefore, the mediation of other people is necessary. Indeed, the self-consciousness humans have requires an external confirmation of their subjectivity: self-consciousness cannot be achieved without another self-consciousness. Yet, other people appear as a threat: the other is the person that may want what I want, and, more broadly, their very presence challenges my impression of reigning over the outside world. The self thus seeks both to destroy the other in order to be the only subject and to obtain recognition from the other.

This leads to the famous struggle of consciousnesses for recognition. According to Hegel, it is possible to represent what happens when two individuals encounter each other as a "struggle to the death." The two individuals want to be recognized as subjects, which creates a struggle for recognition as recognition cannot immediately be mutual. In this struggle, therefore, one individual—who is called the slave or the bondsman, depending on translations—will be afraid to die and will agree to recognize the other in order to preserve her life, whereas the other—the master or the lord—is recognized and gains access to a form of freedom. This struggle to the death is a historical hypothesis that explains how social domination occurs.

However, this lordship is not meant to be unalterable. Hegel has what is called a dialectical understanding of history: each state of social relations can be negated and inverted in a way that will give rise to a new state of social relations (until an "end of history" seen as the triumph of reason is attained). This led Marxist philosophy, and notably the philosopher Alexandre Kojève, to see in the struggle for recognition the framework to propose a narrative of emancipation. Kojève offered an anthropological and Marxist interpretation of it in his courses on Hegel in Paris and called it the "master-slave dialectic." For Kojève, indeed, the situation of the master and the slave at the end of the struggle for recognition is unstable and opens the possibility of an inversion of the situation that would see the slave triumph—which is meant to be a metaphor for the struggle of workers. First, this master-slave relation explains what oppression is. From the moment the slave agrees to recognize the master as a master, oppression functions in the following way: the master conceives of the slave as an other, which means as a being of a nature that is drastically different from his. He puts an end to any possibility of a reciprocal recognition in turning the other subject into a slave. Second, Kojève shows that the struggle for recognition paradoxically situates the slave in a more favorable position than the master. For once he is recognized, the master needs the slave's existence in order for this recognition to persist whereas the slave does not need the master. Moreover, through her work and the transformation of the world she thus undertakes, the slave accesses a form of freedom, independently from the master, to such an extent that Kojève sees in this master-slave dialectic the model to analyze class struggle: the slave creates something through her work, she recognizes herself in this creation, and, thus, she creates new conditions that enable her to take the struggle for recognition up again and to overcome oppression.

THE COMMON FEATURE OF OPPRESSION: OPPRESSED ARE OTHER

Beauvoir uses Hegel's theory of domination and Kojève's reading of it as a tool to bring the general structure of oppression, specifically male domination over women, to light. Beauvoir knew the *Phenomenology of Spirit* well (she read it to distract herself from the anguish of the war during the summer 1940),[3] and she was very familiar with Kojève's analyses. Beauvoir agrees with Hegel that there is an inherent conflictuality in social life. She also agrees that social domination is a process of alienation, which means transforming someone into an other with whom no reciprocity of recognition is possible.

According to Hegelian and post-Hegelian analyses, the other appears to me as an other by comparison to the self that

I am and, more importantly, makes me become aware that I am an "other" for the other. However, everyday life keeps making the relative and reciprocal dimension of this alterity apparent. As Sartre was already showing in his analyses of the gaze, I see that the other perceives herself as a self and perceives me as an other, so I am an other for the other, a self for myself.

Oppression, on the other hand, happens when otherness is not reciprocal, when one group has the power to constitute another group into a group of "others" whose otherness is not the simple, accidental result of their being a different group than the first one but a feature that makes them essentially other. Oppression is therefore what happens when a dominant group manages to constitute a group of the "others," whose alterity—their otherness—is emphasized by a specific meaning given to what differentiates this group. For instance, whites will oppress Blacks in the name of the Black soul, Jews will be oppressed in the name of the Jewish character, women in the name of the eternal feminine.

THE SPECIFICITY OF MALE DOMINATION: WOMAN IS THE OTHER

For Beauvoir, the specificity of women's oppression comes from the fact that men's domination over women does not simply transform women into others but into an Other. The capital letter emphasizes that the alterity of the woman is absolute—it cannot disappear and it has always already existed. For Beauvoir, this absolute alterity is intrinsically linked to submission:

> But the other consciousness has an opposing reciprocal claim: traveling, a local is shocked to realize that in

neighboring countries locals view him as a foreigner; between villages, clans, nations, and classes there are wars, potlatches, agreements, treaties, and struggles that remove the absolute meaning from the idea of the Other and bring out its relativity; whether one likes it or not, individuals and groups have no choice but to recognize the reciprocity of their relation. How is it, then, that between the sexes this reciprocity has not been put forward, that one of the terms has been asserted as the only essential one, denying any relativity in regard to its correlative, defining the latter as pure alterity? Why do women not contest male sovereignty? No subject posits itself spontaneously and at once as the inessential from the outset; it is not the Other who, defining itself as Other, defines the One; the Other is posited as Other by the One positing itself as One. But in order for the Other not to turn into the One, the Other has to submit to this foreign point of view. Where does this submission in woman come from?[4]

There is a specificity to the relation between men and women: women are not both subjects and objects, self and other, as all other individuals are. There is no possible reciprocity in alienation. Women not only are seen by men as the Other but also see themselves in this way, and this is both the cause and the consequence of their submission. To the question "What is a woman?" the response is thus "Woman is the Other," and woman is the Other because she submits to man. To fully respond to the question "What is a woman?" is therefore to respond to the question "Where does this submission in woman come from?"

A NON-DIALECTIC RELATION

The absolute character of alterity that is manifested by the capital letter—the Other instead of the other—is crucial, because it implies that there is no possible dialectic, and so no possible evolution, in the relation between men and women.[5] This means that women's oppression cannot be inverted in an emancipatory way similar to the worker in Kojève's analysis. The very high frequency with which Beauvoir identifies woman as a slave to man, who is the master, her references to Hegel, and the fact that she qualifies woman's existence as "dialectic" in many occasions could lead us to think that Beauvoir equates the relationship between man and woman with the master-slave dialectic. However, women's situation makes such a dialectic impossible. In the Hegelian dialectic, the problem of recognition as well as the dialectical movement stem from the initial equality of the individuals. The two individuals are looking for the recognition of the other; one renounces this recognition out of fear of death and grants her recognition to the other, who becomes, by this fact, her master.[6] The dialectical movement is then put in place because the master, who is apparently victorious, stands in the impasse produced by his victory: he is only recognized by the slave; he thus depends on the one he denied as an equal. The slave, however, finds a way to overcome the denegation and the enslavement she endures, namely through work. Through manual labor, she can transform nature and thus emancipate herself from the master and from nature; which is to say, through her work, the slave attains self-consciousness in a way that liberates her and gives her independence whereas the master needs the slave to remain a slave and for himself to remain the master. For Beauvoir, on the contrary, the woman is always already constituted as an inferior:

> There have not always been proletarians: there have always been women; they are women by their physiological structure; as far back as history can be traced, they have always been subordinated to men; their dependence is not the consequence of an event or a becoming, it did not *happen*.[7]

Women's subordination essentially differs from that of Blacks, Jews, and proletarians insofar as it is not the result of an event; it cannot be dated and has always already existed.[8] In this respect, woman is not in an equal original position with man and thus the man-woman relationship cannot be compared to the master-slave relationship in a Hegelian sense.

Work constitutes the second main difference between the woman and the slave. In the Hegelian outline, the relationship between the master and the slave is dialectical because of the role of work in the acquisition of self-consciousness and, therefore, in the possibility for the slave to reverse the negative movement through which they are made an object. Work, especially manual work, is the necessary condition for the possible emancipation of the slave.[9] Yet the woman that Beauvoir writes about, the woman in the sense of the normative social representation of her time, does not work, or rather her work is, first of all, not considered work and, second, does not have the fruitfulness of the slave's manual work. Indeed, as Beauvoir shows in her meticulous descriptions of housework, the work of the married woman does not have an emancipatory dimension because it is only a struggle against negativity:

> Few tasks are more similar to the torment of Sisyphus than those of the housewife; day after day, one must wash dishes, dust furniture, mend clothes that will be dirty, dusty, and torn again tomorrow. The housewife wears herself out running on the spot; she does nothing; she only perpetuates the present; she never gains the sense that she is conquering a positive Good, but struggles indefinitely against Evil. It is a struggle that begins again every day.[10]

Housework has none of the virtues of the work described by Hegel. It is a sheer struggle against the negativity of filth, mess, and destruction, and as such it does not enable the woman to acquire self-consciousness but, on the contrary, entraps her in an immanence, in a repetition that is never a creation and that prevents her from inscribing herself in a free temporality. This difference in nature between positive work, which is the slave's work in Hegel but also work as a liberation in Marx, or work as a project in Sartre, and housework that is labor with no self-consciousness is one of the reasons why Beauvoir views work outside the home as emancipatory for women. As long as they are confined to housework, women are deprived of the possibility of rendering their relationship with men dialectical since they cannot emancipate themselves through work. It is thus clear that woman's relationship with man is not similar to the master-slave dialectic. She is the absolute Other and not an accidental other whose relative alterity can always be returned.

Beauvoir does not use the master-slave dialectic as a philosophical *model* for the way in which the sexes interact but as a *contrasting tool.*[11] Rather than using the Hegelian figures of the master and the slave to stage the inequality between men and women, Beauvoir brings out the contrast between the position of women and that of the Hegelian slave. Indeed, there is no dialectical tension in the relationship between the sexes. Women fail to demand recognition from men. Because women fail to make this demand, it is unlikely that men would become aware of the relative character of women's alterity; it is thus unlikely that the reciprocity that is inevitable according to Beauvoir when two parties demand recognition would be attained. Therefore, men demand recognition, women fail to demand it, and women are thus constructed as the absolute Other.

Beauvoir uses the master-slave dialectic in two ways. First, she uses it as an idiom through which oppression can be conceived—"alterity is a fundamental category of human thought"[12] and oppression consists in the sedimentation or the naturalization of an alterity that is normally always relative and changing. Second, she uses the master-slave dialectic to highlight the originality of women's oppression: this oppression is absolute and static. If the Hegelian dialectic can be an emancipatory logic for the proletariat, it manifests on the contrary the sexual difference as the locus of an insurmountable oppression. In asking what a woman is, Beauvoir immediately finds herself observing that a woman is, in an immediate way, what a man is *not*, that a woman is the absolute Other, and that this alterity has, historically, been the basis of an inferiority. To respond to the question "What is a woman?" therefore implies shedding light on this intuitive passage, from "woman" to "alterity," to "inferiority," to "submission." The issue of woman's submission is thus the central question of the book. It takes the form of a paradox: How is it possible to explain that women, who are human beings just as men are and hence should be able to make themselves subjects just as men do, are not free and are subjugated to men?

The Woman-Object

If woman's situation is one of specific oppression, it is not only because her alterity is absolute and, in that way, prevents her from accessing an emancipatory dialectic. The other specificity of women's situation lies in the fact that women are not constituted as Other as a social group in the way Blacks, Jews, and proletarians are but as individuals. And the way they are constituted as other happens through objectification.

LIVING WITH THE OPPRESSOR

First, women are not a minority or a marginalized group and, as we have seen, their subordination does not result from a single event or period of history; it has no beginning.[13] Second, unlike Blacks, Jews, or proletarians, they do not live with each other, they live with their oppressors:

> They live dispersed among men, tied by homes, work, economic interests, and social conditions to certain men—father or husband—more closely than to other women. As bourgeois women, they are in solidarity with bourgeois men and not with proletarian women; as white women, they are in solidarity with white men and not with black women.[14] . . . A woman could not even dream of exterminating males. The

tie that binds her to her oppressors is unlike any other. The division of the sexes is a biological given, not a moment in human history. Their opposition took shape within an original Mitsein, and it has not broken it. The couple is a fundamental unit with the two halves riveted to each other: no cleavage of society by sex is possible. This is the fundamental characteristic of woman: she is the Other at the heart of a whole whose two components are necessary to each other.[15]

Male domination is unique in that it takes place in interpersonal relationships whereas most of the other large structures of social domination consist in a domination of one group over an other. The group of women is only a group through misuse of language: women do not share a group identity, there is no solidarity in the name of the group, and there is no group sociability. Women identify with, stick together with, and are socialized with men, inside the family.

In referring here to the Heideggerian concept of *Mitsein* (literally in German "being-with"), Beauvoir complicates her understanding of sexual difference. The being-with refers, in Heidegger, to the idea that Dasein is originally in a world that is (harmoniously) shared with others. Humans are always already in a world in which they are man or woman and in which they are with others. According to Beauvoir, the consequences of this are, first, that the relationship between men and women is not historical and thus is not meant to dramatically change and, second, that women will never be a social group: in their immense majority they live with men and they see their relationship with men as the primary one that defines their group membership.

This use of the concept of being-with is interesting in its ambiguity: on the one hand, it seems to substantiate a certain pessimism. If women are born in a world in which sexual difference is already understood as a sign of their inferiority and if they always live with men, it is hard to see how gender inequalities could disappear. On the other hand, it tempers the agonistic—conflictual—conception of interpersonal relationships that the Hegelian struggle of consciousnesses was illustrating. As Nancy Bauer shows, Beauvoir appeals to Hegel and Heidegger in such a way that instead of opposing them, she holds them together in order to open the possibility of a reciprocal recognition.[16] There is indeed a contradiction between the primary harmony of the being-with and the primary hostility of the struggle for recognition, and Beauvoir argues, in the introduction, for the insufficiency of the Heideggerian approach:

> These phenomena could not be understood if human reality were solely a Mitsein based on solidarity and friendship. On the contrary, they become clear if, following Hegel, a fundamental hostility to any other consciousness is found in consciousness itself; the subject posits itself only in opposition; it asserts itself as the essential and sets up the other as inessential, as the object.[17]

The phenomenon of alterity cannot be explained from the harmony of the being-with. At the same time, the Kojèvian understanding of the struggle for recognition makes a harmonious recognition and therefore the possibility of a harmonious and happy relationship between men and women inconceivable. In holding together Heidegger and Hegel, Beauvoir unveils the possibility of an overcoming—a sublation, in Hegelian terms—of the hostility of consciousnesses toward a reciprocal recognition. The problem to be solved is thus the following: How can we understand what, for the time being, makes this reciprocal recognition impossible and thus confines woman in an absolute alterity?

WOMEN'S OBJECTIFICATION

As we have seen, the common characteristic of all oppressions is alienation—the transformation of the oppressed into an other that is irreducibly different from the self. In male domination, the alienation lived by women occurs through their objectification, that is, their transformation into an object, especially a sexual object. Men conceive of themselves as subjects and conceive of women as objects, beings that are absolutely inferior to them and destined to be used by them. According to Beauvoir, woman is trapped in an absolute alterity because she is objectified by men for whom she is an object of love and an object of desire.

Beauvoir's central thesis about the way women are oppressed by men is that the myth of the Eternal Feminine, that is, the myth of woman as an object of love, allows men to access their humanity without taking the risk of mutual recognition. The only way to overcome the struggle of consciousnesses and the creation of the categories of slave and master on an interpersonal level is friendship. Friendship, which happens when two consciousnesses manage to recognize each other, is apparently the only authentic path, but it requires an authenticity and a generosity that are both hard to reach and dangerous.

But friendship and generosity, which accomplish this recognition of freedoms concretely, are not easy virtues; they are undoubtedly man's highest accomplishment; this is where he is in his truth: but this truth is a struggle endlessly begun, endlessly abolished; it demands that man surpass himself at each instant. . . . But he does not like difficulty; he is afraid of danger. He has contradictory aspirations to both life and rest, existence and being; he knows very well that "a restless spirit" is the ransom for his development, that his distance from the object is the ransom for his being present to himself; but he dreams of restfulness in restlessness and of an opaque plenitude that his consciousness would nevertheless still inhabit. This embodied dream is, precisely, woman; she is the perfect intermediary between nature that is foreign to man and the peer who is too identical to him. She pits neither the hostile silence of nature nor the hard demand of a reciprocal recognition against him; by a unique privilege she is a consciousness, and yet it seems possible to possess her in the flesh. Thanks to her, there is a way to escape the inexorable dialectic of the master and the slave that springs from the reciprocity of freedoms.[18]

The construction of woman as the Other thus appears as an ideal way to escape the difficulties and dangers of mutual recognition while obtaining a recognition of one's freedom. Men have the power to construct women as the type of beings that are sufficiently similar to them to have the ability to recognize them as freedoms and sufficiently different to not pretend to get mutual recognition. Woman is thus conceived as an ideal intermediary between man and animal, which allows men to escape the animal existence of those whose freedom is not recognized by another without having to make the constant effort of wisdom and generosity that mutual recognition requires.

The reason why this figure of the woman as an intermediary is important to understand Beauvoir's analysis of oppression is that woman is made an intermediary in being made an *object* of love and desire. As Beauvoir demonstrates in the "Myths" section, mythical thought transforms singular women in instances of the myth of the Eternal Feminine, that is, the myth of a unique and fixed nature of The Woman, whose function and destiny is to be possessed by the man. In this myth, the woman is mother, prostitute, or virgin, but in any case she is indubitably and absolutely other than the man and petrified in her absolute otherness and immanence to the extent that nothing can be said of her:

> It can be said that a peasant woman is a good or bad worker, that an actress has or does not have talent: but if a woman is considered in her immanent presence, absolutely nothing can be said about that, she is outside of the realm of qualification. Now, in amorous or conjugal relations and in all relations where woman is the vassal, the Other, she is grasped in her immanence. It is striking that the woman friend, colleague, or associate is without mystery.[19]

Not only does love petrify woman in an otherness that excludes her from the world of concrete human beings, but love functions as a screen that hides the material dimensions of women's oppression. One of the key mechanisms of the oppression of women and of its perpetuation consists in making it look like an individual problem and not a structural and social issue. Through the idea of feminine mystery, what is hidden is the fact that women's passivity and their mystery are direct consequences of the patriarchal organization of society and law. For instance, Beauvoir shows in the last chapter of the "Myths" section that "as man holds a privileged place in this world, he is the one who is able actively to display his love; very often he keeps the woman, or at least he helps her out; in marrying her, he gives her social status; he gives her gifts; his economic and social independence permits his endeavors and innovations."[20] Because men work outside the home, because they inherit, and because they have a salary, they can act, take initiative; the housewife and the young woman waiting for her suitor are in a passive position created by the social and legal organization of the world in which they live. Women's passivity is presented as a feature of women's nature and as their choice or preference when it is first and foremost the result of their structural oppression.

It is thus in the name of love that women are transformed into a mythical and mysterious Other, of whom nothing can be said and whose otherness seems historical and essential. The otherness of woman turns her into an object of passion as much as rejection, an adored other that is made essentially different and inaccessible by this adoration. This role of love gives women's oppression an original, paradoxical, and particularly difficult character. Indeed, on the one hand love creates a sexual difference that constitutes a basis for women's oppression by men, but on the other hand it creates an original situation in which oppressors love the oppressed and the oppressed love their oppressors. For men, woman is not or not only an object to consume or destroy but also an object to love. For women, this love, which can't be dissociated from the objectification it creates, makes oppression bearable if not justifiable. In both cases, the role played by love in women's oppression makes this oppression hard to pinpoint and even harder to avoid: it is indeed hard to see love as a source of oppression, and the pleasures of love make the oppression it induces very appealing.

OBJECTIFICATION AND OBJECTIVITY

The objectification of women has significant consequences for the organization of society and of knowledge: Beauvoir brings to light the link between objectivity, gaze, and objectification. She thus writes, at the beginning of the part devoted to myths:

> Woman is sometimes designated as "the sex"; it is she who is the flesh, its delights and its dangers. That for woman it is man who is sexed and carnal is a truth that has never been proclaimed because there is no one to proclaim it. The representation of the world as the world itself is the work of men; they describe it from a point of view that is their own and that they confound with the absolute truth.[21]

The male standpoint has the specificity of conceiving itself as neutral and thus neutralizes women's objectification, whereas it is not objective but results in male domination. Catharine MacKinnon quotes this passage as the starting point of her claim that objectivity is constructed from the male gaze, that is, a gaze that objectifies women:

> Men *create* the world from their own point of view, which then *becomes* the truth to be described. . . . *Power to create*

> *the world from one's point of view is power in its male form.*
> The male epistemological stance, which corresponds to the
> world it creates, is objectivity: the ostensibly noninvolved
> stance, the view from a distance and from no particular per-
> spective, apparently transparent to its reality. It does not
> comprehend its own perspectivity, does not recognize what
> it sees as subject like itself, or that the way it apprehends its
> world is a form of its subjugation and presupposes it. The
> objectivity knowable is object. Woman through male eyes
> is sex object, that by which man knows himself at once as
> man and as subject.[22]

Women's situation cannot be dissociated from the objectification that male eyes impose on them, and male domination enables this objectification to go unnoticed and to make
women's submission look like their objective condition, not
the result of men's domination.

Because of male domination, two truths about women contradict themselves: they are both human beings, so free in their
essence, and constructed by male eyes as essentially inferior
and thus destined to submission. At the end of the introduction
of *The Second Sex*, both the main issue and the organization of
the book appear clearly: responding to the question "What is
a woman?" is shedding light on the tension between woman's
freedom qua human being and her submission qua woman:

> What singularly defines woman's situation is that being,
> like all humans, an autonomous freedom, she discovers and
> chooses herself in a world where men force her to assume
> herself as the Other: an attempt is made to freeze her as an
> object and doom her to immanence, since her transcendence

will be forever transcended by another essential and sovereign consciousness. Woman's drama lies in this conflict between the fundamental claim of every subject, which always posits itself as essential, and the demands of a situation that constitutes her as inessential. How, in the feminine condition, can a human being accomplish herself? What paths are open to her? Which ones lead to dead ends? How can she find independence within dependence? What circumstances limit women's freedom and can she overcome them? These are the fundamental questions we would like to elucidate. This means that in focusing on the individual's possibilities, we will define these possibilities not in terms of happiness but in terms of freedom.[23]

In order to understand this tension, the analysis must elucidate what allows femininity to be constructed, through women's objectification, as the absolute alterity and how this construction structures women's submission. Women's submission is their condition in the sense that it is the possibility that is made available to them by the social norm. And the analysis will have to shed light on what makes this submission appear as a destiny, how it perpetuates itself, and what the respective roles of men and women are in this perpetuation. Beauvoir's fundamental thesis, which she deploys throughout the book, can thus be reformulated in the following way: "One is not born, but rather becomes, a submissive woman."

7

The Objectified Body of
the Submissive Woman

We saw in the previous chapter that patriarchy, that is, the social oppression of women by men, occurs through the transformation of women into an absolute Other, whose function is to be an object of love and desire for men. This analysis of oppression may seem theoretical and abstract. In reality, it permeates all aspects of women's lives and explains how and why they submit to men and to patriarchal norms. A good example of the concrete character of women's alienation through objectification is the way in which it impacts the experience that women have of their own bodies. To show how women, even though they are not born in such a way, become submissive if they do not resist the norms of femininity, Beauvoir draws attention to the ways in which femininity, and therefore submission, are inscribed in the body. Specifically, Beauvoir shows that women are the only beings whose bodies already have a social meaning before they can even experience them. That is to say, becoming a woman is discovering that our own body belongs to men's gaze even before it is fully ours. The specificity of woman's body, according to Beauvoir, is that it is a social body before being a lived body and therefore functions as a destiny.

Woman Cannot Abstract Herself from Her Body

From the very beginning of *The Second Sex*, Beauvoir claims that the body and embodiment in general are of decisive importance to address her main question, "What is a woman?" According to her, it is impossible to answer such a question without recognizing (1) that men and women both *are* and *have* bodies, and (2) that an important dimension of sex difference is to be found in the fact that women, unlike men, cannot escape their bodies and their social meaning.[1]

A dominant theory about the body in the philosophical tradition since Plato has been dualism, understood as the thesis that the body and the soul are essentially different. Beauvoir, like many philosophers of the phenomenological tradition, challenges this hypothesis and the underlying assumption it often includes, namely that the soul should be the focus of philosophical analysis. Historically, the phenomenological tradition has discussed and challenged dualism through the way it is built in the philosophy of René Descartes: Husserl's *Cartesian Meditations* are a response to Descartes's *Meditations* and Merleau-Ponty's *Phenomenology of Perception* can be read as a long challenge of Descartes. In a similar manner, as Nancy Bauer has shown, the introduction of *The Second Sex* can be read as a feminine or feminist appropriation of Descartes's philosophical gesture in the *Meditations*. In the second meditation, Descartes wonders what kind of being he is. He relies on evidence and on clear and distinct ideas in order to claim what is self-evident: he is a man, a human being. From there, he builds the following reasoning: since he can doubt the existence of his body but cannot doubt his own existence, then the body cannot be an essential element of what it is to be a human being. In a similar manner, Beauvoir opens *The Second Sex* with an autobiographical justification of her writing. However, this justification consists in saying that when she is asked to define herself, her first response, the one she thinks she "must" give on the face of it, is that she is a woman.[2] And this comes from the fact that, unlike Descartes, she cannot doubt the existence of her body nor abstract herself from it. To be a woman is, in part, to be unable to escape the fact that you are a body.

Beauvoir agrees with non-dualist philosophers like Merleau-Ponty that men and women are not dual substances and that they both are and have their body. But she does not limit herself to a simple objection to the Cartesian idea of a difference of nature between the body and the soul, that is, to dualism: if it were simply that the soul is not distinct from the body, there would be no specificity of women's body. Neither men nor women could, in such a context, doubt the existence of their body. She shows, however, that only women see their identity designated by their body: they cannot pretend, like Descartes does, that they are not bodies. For Merleau-Ponty, for instance, it is not possible to escape our body in the sense that our body is our hold on the world, but this is not a preexisting norm imposed by society on a person. The body is the condition for the being-in-the-world of the person, but it is not a fixed destiny.

This conception of the body is central in order to clarify the mystery of female submission and to understand both how woman is conceived as the Other and why she does not demand to be recognized as a subject. The social dimension of women's bodies structures their situation and their experience in such a way that submission appears to them as a destiny, that is, both as a path already mapped out and as what they should do. A very concrete example of this can be found in Iris Marion Young's "Throwing Like a Girl."[3] Young studies the ways in which patriarchal norms prevent women from taking as much space as men, convince them of their weakness, and teach them to fear being perceived as inviting sexual objectification and, therefore, constrain women's bodies in such a way that they can only "throw like a girl."

This thesis of a preeminence of the social body over the lived body—that is, the idea that woman's body is a body that appears to others, that is looked at by others, before being a body lived by the woman—is inseparable from a challenge of the Sartrean individualism. For Sartre, there is bad faith from the moment a person acts as if they were an object moved by the world, as if they were determined by the world, because in reality they are absolutely free to make choices and to create their own projects. On the contrary, Beauvoir proposes a philosophy of the body in which the social dimension of women's bodies structures the situation and the experience of women in such a way that they are destined to submit themselves. In order to establish this, Beauvoir adopts a phenomenological approach that enables her to show that the objectification of women is at the root of their submission. Specifically, Beauvoir's analysis of woman's body reveals that there are four dimensions of this body: it is a physiological body, a lived body, an accidentally objectified body, and a body lived as already structurally objectified.

The Biological Body Is Social

Beauvoir opens *The Second Sex* with a study of the physiological body through the biological differences between males and females, especially but not only in the human species. Even if many of her scientific data and theories are outdated, the heart of her argument remains relevant. Her line of reasoning is the following: there are biological differences between males and females; these differences are such that females are less strong than males; and females are "subordinat[ed] to the species"[4] when biology does not come in the way of males' independence.

WOMEN ARE ALIENATED BY THEIR BODIES

Beauvoir shows that women's relation to their physiological body creates a sense of alienation. At the level of the physiological body women are already subordinated, but this is not a submission to man: the physiological body subordinates her to the species. Men, like women, have a physiological body. At that level, there are thus no power relations between men and women; they only have different physical attributes. On the other hand, there is a form of subordination that is specific to women, what Beauvoir calls "woman's enslavement to the species."[5] If men can be pure individuals in the sense that the perpetuation of the species does not require that they go against the demands of their individuality,[6] the perpetuation of the species requires that women negate their individuality. According to Beauvoir, there are parts of women's bodies that have no purpose for the individual (mammary glands, for instance); there are moments in a woman's life where she works for the species and against herself, and "there is no way to escape that tyranny because it enslaves individual life at the same time that it nourishes it."[7] Beauvoir writes that "gestation is tiring work that offers woman no benefit as an individual but that demands serious sacrifices,"[8] be it because of the nausea and fatigue or the progressive restriction of movement. If many readers have reproached Beauvoir for her blindness to the benefits and the pleasures of pregnancy and breastfeeding, her argument remains nonetheless valid: these experiences manifest a conflict between individuality, which demands movement, expending energy, personal projects, and a form of selfishness, and procreation, which requires putting oneself at the service of a future being.

This enslavement to the species, which she also calls "subordination"[9] and "servitude,"[10] creates a simple difference between men and women and, in this respect, does not explain why women submit to men. Yet, according to Beauvoir, women's physiological body produces an inner division and conflict: menstruation, pregnancy, and breastfeeding are presented as moments of a "conflict between the species and the individual"[11] where woman is negated in her individuality by her own body. Because of these moments, "woman *is* her body as man *is* his, but her body is something other than her."[12] Her body is where the species perpetuates itself, but this perpetuation happens to the detriment of the individual. Woman's embodiment is such that the classical, masculine model of a disembodied subject that would reign over his body cannot apply to her: an important part of what it is to be a woman is to be a body.

THE SOCIAL CHARACTER OF THE PHYSIOLOGICAL BODY

Some commentators,[13] in using this argument, have made the mistake of believing that Beauvoir is defending a biological determinism. On the contrary, she affirms at the end of the chapter she devotes to biology that biological differences do not matter as such; they only matter from the moment they are socially defined as important:

> A society is not a species: in it the species realizes itself as existence; it transcends itself toward the world and the future; its customs cannot be deduced from biology; individuals are never left to their nature; they obey this second nature, that is customs, in which the desires and fears that express their ontological attitude are reflected. It is not as a body but as a body subjected to taboos and laws that the subject gains consciousness of and accomplishes themselves: it is in the name of certain values that they valorize themselves. And once again, physiology cannot ground values: rather, biological data take on those values the existent confers to them. If the respect or the fear woman inspires prohibits

man from using violence against her, the male's muscular superiority is not a source of power.[14]

We have a tendency to infer from women's physical weakness a "natural" reason for their social inferiority. In reality, the physiological body itself does not carry a signification; it does not mean anything on its own, but it supports social meanings. If women are indeed physically weaker than men on average, this inferiority is significant only if society grants it value—in a society that does not attach importance to physical strength, this difference between men and women would not matter.

In sum, women's physiological body matters on two levels: first, because it is the physiological basis of the way women live their body, and second, because of the signification that is attached to it through social norms:

> It is thus in the light of an ontological economic, social, and psychological context that we will have to clarify the biological data. Woman's enslavement to the species, the limits of her individual abilities, are facts of extreme importance; the woman's body is one of the essential elements of the situation she occupies in this world. But her body is not enough to define her; it has a lived reality only as taken on by consciousness through actions and within a society; biology alone cannot provide an answer to the question that concerns us: why is woman the Other? The question is how, in her, nature has been taken on in the course of history; the question is what humanity has made of the human female.[15]

In order to understand what a woman is, a philosophy of the body is thus necessary, as well as a consideration of woman's physiological body. That being said, one thing should remain clear: the physiological body does not shape women's destiny; it only *supports* a destiny that is socially constituted and that is then naturalized in the body. Women's destiny is socially constituted, but it is inscribed in the physiological body and supported by it. In the conclusion of the book, Beauvoir proposes a thought experiment in which she shows that a non-sexist education of girls would completely change the signification and thus the experience they have of their biological bodies: instead of experiencing disgust and anguish, as Beauvoir describes in the chapters on "childhood" and "the girl," and which is a result in part of the dissonance between the lived body and the objectified body that we will study in what follows, girls would peacefully undergo and get through puberty.[16] Thus women's bodies cannot be fully understood by merely describing what they are like from the outside—one must understand what it is like to live in them.

A Lived Body That Can Be Objectified: What Men and Women Have in Common

Beauvoir refutes the idea that biology could be the basis for women's inferiority, but she nevertheless recognizes the significance of the body in shaping women's social situation. In order to shed light on this, she appropriates a distinction between the physiological body and the lived body that she inherits from the phenomenological tradition. According to Husserl, as we saw, phenomenology must describe and analyze the body as a lived experience. Merleau-Ponty, a phenomenologist and one of Beauvoir's closest friends, shows that studying the body implies analyzing the way in which our body appears to us and how we experience it. According to him, the main commitment of phenomenology consists in going back to what he calls a "prescientific life of the consciousness."[17] Applied to the body, it means that, in order to understand what the body is, we need to go back to "the body itself"—that is, the body as we experience it and as it appears to us—before we even begin to have a theoretical and scientific knowledge of it. Cartesian dualism and the subject/object dichotomy that is in its very principle rooted in this dualism render it impossible to understand the reality of the experience of the body, which is the experience of a union between me and the world. The body is not something we own; it is our general medium for having a world.

THE LIVED BODY

Beauvoir adopts this Merleau-Pontian understanding of the lived body. She thus writes, "In the perspective I adopt—that of Heidegger, Sartre, and Merleau-Ponty—if the body is not a *thing*, it is a situation: it is our grasp on the world and the outline for our projects."[18] And later, "It is not the body-object described by scientists that exists concretely but the body lived by the subject."[19] She refuses to understand the body as a thing. Women, like men, are situated by how they live their body. Their body is one of the means through which the world always already has meaning for individuals since it is the medium through which they grasp the world.

The lived body, insofar as it is the subjective experience of the physiological body, differs from one individual to the next. It would even be possible to say that lived bodies are incomparable from one individual to another. The lived body is the experience of *being* a body and not only of *having* a body. However, since "the body is the instrument of our hold on the world,"[20] the differences among physiological bodies generate differences in the way the body is lived and the world is perceived. While men see their body as a tool to climb, to play, or to explore the world, women often perceive their body as a weight, as a source of pain, or as a risk (of unwanted pregnancy, for instance). Female bodies' enslavement to the species thus has consequences on women's lived bodies and on their perception of the world. This point appears clearly when Beauvoir briefly describes the consequences of menopause:

> So woman finds herself freed from the servitudes of the female; she is not comparable to a eunuch, because her vitality is intact; however, she is no longer prey to powers that submerge her: she coincides with herself.[21]

This argument emphasizes, by contrast, to what extent women, through menstruation, pregnancy, and breastfeeding, find themselves alienated from themselves.[22] If menopause can appear as a relief and as coincidence with one true self, it is because the experience women have of their body is the experience of being other, foreign: menstruation gives woman the impression that something is going on in her body that is not her—in the sense that she does not identify with it—and over which she has no control. (This experience of alienation in one's relationship with one's body can of course happen to men during sickness or old age, but this would be considered abnormal; for women, such an experience corresponds to their normal embodiment.) Woman lives pregnancy "both as an enrichment and a mutilation; the fetus is part of her body, and it is a parasite exploiting her; she possesses it, and she is possessed by it."[23] Moreover, she knows—even though the risks are much lower today than they were in Beauvoir's lifetime—that this alienation of the pregnancy can culminate in her death or the child's death during delivery. Likewise, breastfeeding is an "exhausting servitude"[24] that puts woman's body at the disposal of the child.

This alienation has two major consequences. First, women are divided in their relation to their own body. A woman cannot fully consider her body as her own: "she feels . . . that her body is an alienated opaque thing; it is the prey of a stubborn and foreign life."[25] Second, it makes woman's life ambiguous: she is at the same time a subject—and as such she *has* her body at the same time as she *is* her body—and she does *not* have her body, since this body can appear to her as being against her or as belonging to the child.

For Beauvoir, the ambiguous experience women have of their biological bodies is not what explains their submission. Yet, in a way this experience prepares them for or is the basis of conceiving of themselves as passive beings moved by exterior forces, as alienated beings. This appears clearly when one analyzes the vocabulary Beauvoir uses in the last pages of the chapter titled "Biological Data" and in the pages of the second volume devoted to puberty—which is, in her eyes, the true starting point of submission. In both cases, woman is depicted as conceiving of herself as a "prey";[26] she experiences her "alienation";[27] she is "passive."[28] In resorting to the lexical fields of servitude ("servitude," "slave," "enslavement," "submission") in both cases, Beauvoir underlines the analogy between the experience of alienation in the physiological body and in the experience of puberty, meaning in the lived body. It is the coexistence of this alienation created by the physiological body alongside the socially produced objectification, however, that makes it possible for submission to occur.

THE BODY AS AN OBJECT

Beauvoir uses Merleau-Ponty's distinction between the body-object and the lived body and Sartre's considerations on the way the other transforms my body into an object to build her own original analysis of woman's body. If Merleau-Ponty rejects the subject/object opposition and structures his philosophy of the body around this rejection, for Sartre, the body is the paradigmatic location of objectification.

Sartre's understanding of embodied objectification is complex, yet it is central to understanding Beauvoir's theory of embodied oppression and, therefore, her account of female submission. In *Being and Nothingness*, the philosophy of the body is inseparable from the conception of alterity—from the way Sartre conceives of social relations as antagonistic relationships with others. Sartre leans on Hegel to view interpersonal relations as a "conflict of consciousnesses." Each individual is, first, alone and isolated—what Sartre calls a being-for-itself, present to itself—and is marked by a facticity he has to transcend: we are all born in a certain place, of certain parents, at a certain date, but being a human is being able to overcome those facts in exercising our freedom. In a second phase, the individual experiences the existence of others. This experience is immediately presented as a negative one by Sartre. He conceives of shame[29] as a paradigmatic manifestation of this negative experience. Sartre thus summarizes the appearance of an other:

> He is the one who is other than I; therefore he is given as a non-essential object with a character of negativity. But this Other is also a self-consciousness. As such he appears to me as an ordinary object immersed in the being of life. Similarly it is thus that I appear to the Other: as a concrete, sensible, immediate existence.[30]

Sartre proposes an individual and phenomenological understanding of the struggle for recognition. In reality, the Other appears first as "eyes,"[31] as a gaze that sees me and transforms me into a being-looked-at. In this respect, the Other is not first perceived as an object but as a gaze that makes me an object.[32] He uncovers for me my being-for-others.

The gaze of the Other thus leads me to perceive my body as a body-for-others, that is, as an object, and I perceive the bodies of others as so many objects. The relationship with the Other makes me distinguish between my body-for-myself and my body-for-others. For Sartre, the first experience I have of my body is the experience of my body-for-myself, that is, of my body as a consciousness. And the relationship with an other transforms my body into a body-for-others. It is thus very important that, for Sartre, the body does not appear as what it *is*, that is, for the fact it is crucial in my being-for-myself; it does not appear for the subject. It only becomes the topic of an interrogation because of the struggle with the other: "This object which the Other is for me and this object which I am for him are manifested each *as* a body. What then is my body? What is the body of the Other?"[33] I start wondering about my body and my body appears to me as being "my body" only from the moment I experience the other.[34]

Through the encounter with the other, the body appears divided between two completely different experiences: my body is either the body-for-itself, which is my body as I apprehend it myself, or the body-for-other, which is an object.[35] Sartre is not interested in the way I experience my own body, what allows me to grasp the world—that is, as the medium that allows me to seize and perceive the world—nor in the way the other's body appears to me. The other indeed appears not as a body but as a look or as a mere presence (for instance, the movement in the branches of a tree or the steps in a corridor) that produces my being-looked-at and makes me become aware of the way my body becomes a body-for-others.

The body-for-itself is what I am, it is inseparable from my presence in the world and, to that extent, I do not have it, I am it; it is not an object for me;[36] it manifests my facticity. This immediacy of my relationship with my body is negated by the encounter with the other, which makes me understand that my body is for him something exterior, an object. The body-for-others is my body insofar as it is objectified by an other and thus insofar as it is alienated, in the sense that it is made other than what it is for me and that it belongs in a certain sense to the other and not to be: "the body-for-the-other is the body-for-us, but inapprehensible and alienated";[37] it is the body that makes me shy, the body I am ashamed of. These two bodies cannot be reduced to one another, and Sartre rejects a unified conception of the body, through which the body-for-us and the body-for-the-other would be lived as a single reality.

The body-for-the-other is an experience of alienation that is unbearable for the subject: in objectifying me through his look, the other possesses me. This alienation of objectification makes conflict with the other inevitable:

> Everything which may be said of me in my relations with the Other applies to him as well. While I attempt to free myself from the hold of the Other, the Other is trying to free himself from mine; while I seek to enslave the Other, the Other seeks to enslave me. We are by no means dealing with unilateral relations with an object-in-itself, but with reciprocal and moving relations. The following descriptions of concrete behavior must therefore be envisaged within the perspective of conflict. Conflict is the original meaning of being-for-others.[38]

This conflictual relation with the other is central in Sartre's philosophy of the body: the relation with the other is an alienating relation of objectification, and I necessarily fight with the other in order to counter the alienation he makes me experience and, thus, in order to maintain my status as a subject.

The Alienation of Women: The Objectified Lived Body

The central role objectification plays in Beauvoir's philosophy of the body leads her to distinguish two specifically feminine experiences of the body. First, women's bodies are objectified on a social level to such an extent that this objectification preexists the experience that women can have of their own bodies. Second, this structural objectification determines the experience that women can have of their own bodies to the extent that only women have an experience of the lived body as objectified.

THE OBJECTIFICATION OF WOMEN IS SOCIAL

The fact that men turn women into objects to be loved, to be sexually consummated, or to be used for free domestic work impacts the way women live in their bodies. The first volume of *The Second Sex* shows that one of the ways in which men affirm that they are subjects is in conceiving women as objects and treating them as such. Women are considered objects to be exchanged in marriage and kinship, as the anthropologist Claude Lévi-Strauss showed; women are transformed into objects of desire in myths and literature. In the part she devotes to myths, Beauvoir establishes that the constant objectification of women in myths is a constant objectification of their body: the female body is considered sometimes as prey, sometimes as a source of disgust, sometimes as property. In any case, men constitute an image of themselves as subjects, as heroes, and as warriors in making women's body an object. To phrase it differently, women are made into objects in such a way that men covet desirable women in the same way they covet treasures.

We saw earlier that Beauvoir adopts a theory of interpersonal relations, that is, the one developed by Hegel and endorsed by Sartre, in which there is an inherent conflict between human beings such that two individuals are engaged in a "conflict of consciousnesses"[39] in which they are at once subjects (being-for-oneself) and objects (being-for-the-other): each individual sees himself as a subject and sees the other as an object, thus they are both subjects and objects. Yet the social structure of gender inequality allows men to systematically define themselves as subjects in defining women as objects. Women, therefore, are not at once subjects and objects; they are first and foremost being-for-others, for men. Patriarchy structures the difference between men and women in such a way that men are subjects (they do things) while women are objects (to be possessed and used by men). To be a woman is not only to have a woman's body and to live in it; it is also to have a social body that is objectified. Male and female bodies alike can be objectified in interpersonal relations, but this objectification is contingent—it does not have to happen—and is reciprocal. For instance, one way to describe what occurs during sex is that each partner is using the other partner's body as an object for sexual satisfaction.[40] When this happens between equal partners, the objectification is accidental, temporary, and reciprocal—each partner is an object for the other partner. By contrast, the social structure of gender inequality grants power to men such that this accidental objectification becomes structural and precedes the lived experience of the body: while men are subjects first and, through the other's gaze, can discover themselves as objects, women are objects first. Therefore, a woman's body is objectified before she can experience it as her own lived body.

The very fact that women are alienated in their lived body does not suffice to constitute them as Others: it is through men's gaze that women are frozen in an alterity they cannot escape. In nondominant interpersonal relationships, the other appears to me as an other by contrast to the self that I am. Yet everyday life constantly emphasizes the relative dimension of this alterity: I can easily see that the other perceives himself as a self and perceives me as an other. This relativity of alterity is further reinforced by exchanges at the social group level: when I travel abroad, I see that I am a foreigner to those living in the countries I visit and that I am, in that way, transformed into an object in a manner similar to the objectification of foreigners I observe when I am not one. This reciprocal, mundane form of othering can be morally neutral because of the consciousness subjects have of its reciprocal character.

By contrast, Beauvoir highlights the specific, and morally wrong, form of objectification and othering that occurs in patriarchy through her distinction between "the other" and "the Other." Woman is constituted by man as the Other and not just an other, at the individual level as well as the social level, that is to say, as an absolute and non-relative alterity. The specificity of women's objectification appears clearly: to say that the woman is the Other is to emphasize that she is precisely not included in the reciprocity of alterity. Her alterity is absolute, excludes her from any reciprocity, and is the basis of her objectification. Through the example of Eve, Beauvoir shows that woman is conceived as "a simple accident," "in the inessential mode" and a "naturally submissive consciousness."[41] This inessential, non-threatening status is justified by woman's dual nature:

> She is the ideal intermediary between nature that is foreign to man and the peer who is too identical to him. She pits neither the hostile silence of nature nor the hard demand of a reciprocal recognition against him; by a unique privilege she is a consciousness, and yet it seems possible to possess her in the flesh.[42]

Men, thanks to their social power, managed to make woman an Other, that is to say to treat her as a particularly ambiguous being, conscious enough to recognize men as subjects and, at the same time, similar to an object through her body. In that way, according to Beauvoir, male domination consists in assigning to women the destiny of being the type of being whose body is an object and therefore whose body is flesh. An extreme example of this phenomenon that comes immediately to mind is the way in which the cinematography of pornography means to show women's bodies as many organs to be used and holes to be penetrated. In front of this destiny, submission stands out as the path to follow.

THE BODY IS AN OBJECT BEFORE BEING LIVED

Because the objectification of women's bodies is inscribed in the social structure, it preexists the experience that any woman can have of her own body. In that sense, it calls for another distinction. In the same way that human beings have a physiological body and that the experience they have of it makes it a lived body, women have an objectified body and the experience they have of it constitutes a lived objectified body.

This idea is deeply different from the body-for-the-other: the objectification of women's bodies does not begin with interpersonal relationships; it is something that precedes them. Beauvoir clearly makes this claim in her analysis of puberty at the beginning of the second volume. According to Beauvoir, puberty occurs when the girl's body becomes "flesh."[43] This transformation is obviously a transformation of the physiological body. But the detailed description Beauvoir gives of it at the end of the first chapter of the second volume ("Childhood") argues that puberty is a transition from one lived body to another and that this transition happens through the awareness of her body as an objectified one: "Under her sweater, under her blouse, her breasts are spreading and this body that the little girl identified with self appears to her as flesh; it is an object that others look at and see."[44] Becoming flesh does not happen through an evolution of the physiological body; it is the transition from one lived body to another. Indeed, "flesh" is the woman's body insofar as it is seen as an object of desire by the male gaze. Becoming flesh thus implies becoming looked at in a sexual and lustful way.

Beauvoir then describes a largely shared experience of puberty: becoming flesh occurs through the shock in the discovery that one is being looked at. Beauvoir quotes a woman who says, in recounting her first experience of hearing a comment made by a stranger in the street about her body when she was thirteen: "I will never forget the shock I suddenly felt in seeing myself seen."[45] From puberty onward, woman will experience a body that is objectified before it can be a body-for-myself: in public spaces and in family interactions, a girl will suddenly understand that her body is sexualized by men's look. While until then she was not catching anyone's eye, she then sees herself seen, examined, desired. In a certain way, she will have to realize that, with puberty, her body has become something that does not belong to her anymore, that is not her own body anymore but a *woman*'s body—that is, in men's eyes, an object of desire. This experience of femininity is so common that some sociologists who study street harassment and its consequences on teenage girls still consider these pages of *The Second Sex* as the best summary of the phenomenon today.[46] Even today, puberty is lived as a transition from body to flesh, through which a girl becomes aware that her body is not primarily *her* body but what makes her appear in the world as possible prey.

This transition demonstrates that the temporality of the lived body is reversed for women and for women only. Even before a young girl becomes fully a woman and starts living her woman's body, this body has the social signification of a sexual object. Her body-for-herself is first a body-for-the-other, a body that signals her as being likely to be sexually possessed. Instead of being in the situation described by Sartre, of knowing oneself as a subject and then discovering oneself as an object for the other, when a girl experiences street harassment or sexualized comments on her changing body she is forced to discover herself as an object before she can fully live this new body. This explains why many girls—who reject this new body that attracts bizarre and often incomprehensible attention—react to the changes of their body during puberty with embarrassment and disgust. Another example is the ambivalent relationship that many women have with their breasts: on the one hand, their breasts are a part of their body and a part of themselves; on the other hand, their breasts are a site of a sexualization of their body in which they have no part. Wearing a bra (or not), using sports bras or sexy lace bras, showing some cleavage or hiding the breasts are all decisions that women are socially urged to make. This illustrates that their breasts do not fully belong to them in a double sense: they are sexualized even before the woman can want to conceive of them as erogenous, and they are always presented as for the man who will look at them instead of for the experience—and maybe the pleasure—of the woman herself.

Through this experience of alienation during puberty, and through many other experiences of sexual objectification, Beauvoir reveals one of the central theses of the second volume: to understand what a woman is means to understand what it is to live in the first person (as a subject) in a body that has already been constructed (by man's gaze) as an object.

From the Body-Object to the Passive Prey

Beauvoir's analysis of women's bodies demonstrates that there are four dimensions of this body: it is a physiological body, a lived body, an accidentally objectified body, and a body lived as already structurally objectified. These four dimensions (Sartre's and Merleau-Ponty's accounts have just two) are a consequence of the social order: men's social superiority allows them to construct women as objects and thus to constitute their bodies as objectified, as bodies-for-other before they can even begin being a body-for-herself. This phenomenological account of women's bodies is illuminating in itself and it enables Beauvoir to explain how female submission functions.

Beauvoir indeed shows that men's objectification of women's bodies incites women to conform to this status of the Other that is expected from them. As we noted before, the experience that the teenage girl has of her body makes her feel alienated from this body. The male gaze adds a new layer to this alienation through male comments on this body that she already has a hard time seeing as her own. Through his comments, the man transforms her body into a body for him and not a body for her. Beauvoir provides a detailed description of the distress created by the experience of a body or, more precisely, of a flesh that is always already constructed as an object of desire. This distress leads the girl to lose the hold she had on her body, which means to lose her grasp of being in the world:

The adolescent girl is condemned to the lie of pretending to be object, and a prestigious one, while she experiences herself as an uncertain, dispersed existence, and she knows her failings. Makeup, false curls, corsets, padded bras, are lies; the face itself becomes a mask: spontaneous expressions are produced artfully, a wondrous passivity is imitated; there is nothing more surprising than suddenly discovering in the exercise of one's feminine functions a physiognomy of familiar aspect; its transcendence denies itself and imitates immanence; one's eyes no longer perceive, they reflect; one's body no longer lives: it waits; every gesture and smile becomes an appeal; disarmed, available, the girl is nothing but a flower offered, a fruit to be picked. Man encourages her in these lures by demanding to be lured: then he gets irritated, he accuses. But for the guileless girl, he has nothing but indifference and even hostility. He is only seduced by the one who sets traps for him; offered, she is still the one who stalks her prey; her passivity takes the form of an undertaking, she makes her weakness a tool of her strength; since she is forbidden to attack outright, she is reduced to maneuvers and calculations; and it is in her interest to appear freely given; therefore, she will be criticized for being perfidious and treacherous, and she is. But it is true that she is obliged to offer man the myth of her submission because he insists on dominating.[47]

In this context, the girl perceives that she is flesh (an object for men), a destiny that is hard to escape. She is indeed constantly shown all the benefits she will receive for not resisting her role as prey. Therefore the ambiguity of submission manifests itself: on the one hand, the girl has a certain freedom to choose or to refuse this appealing passivity—she can decide to refuse to make herself a beautiful object for men but she would be seen as abnormal, as unsexy, and she would probably pay a significant price for it. On the other hand, if she were to choose to do as she is told and to make herself beautiful submissive prey, this choice can hardly be seen as a sign of moral vice, since the experience she has of her body as always already objectified gives her good reason to think she has no other choice than being other.

The alienation created by the physiological body as it is lived in the context of male objectification leads women to conceive of themselves as destined to be passive and submissive flesh. Submission is the prescribed and expected behavior. More importantly even, this submission is so embodied in a woman's body that it becomes inseparable from her eroticism: whether Rousseau—who seems to have forgotten, in his condemnation of submission, the pleasure he took in Mlle Lambercier's spanking[48]—liked it or not, submission is not always lived as a renouncement of freedom and sometimes appears as the path to infinite delights.

8

Delights or Oppression: The Ambiguity of Submission

We have seen that women's oppression in patriarchy takes the form of an alienation—of transformation into an Other—that occurs through an objectification and that this objectification has crucial effects on the way women's oppression is inscribed in their bodies. The bodily dimension of women's objectification reveals a close relationship between women's beauty and their objectification: the specificity of a woman's body comes from the fact it is always a body for men, and women's bodies are conceived as passive objects to be consumed by men. However, an ambiguity surfaces: Is it really a form of passivity to make oneself a sexy object for men? Passivity is the opposite of activity, and turning oneself into a sexy object (e.g., by dieting, applying makeup, exercising, or shopping for clothes) requires many actions. But if submission is not passivity, does it mean that women actually choose it? If so, why would they? Again,

Beauvoir shows us a way to solve this problem: submission can be *pleasurable*.

The second volume of *The Second Sex* can be read as a long description of all the forms that women's submission takes and the degree to which submitting can seem tempting. From the perspective of our inquiry, the most important and simultaneously the most taboo point that Beauvoir brings to light is the following: there is, for woman, something pleasant in submission. This does not mean that women are naturally destined to submission—quite the contrary. Beauvoir shows that the pleasure taken in submission stems from woman's specific situation. It does not mean that submission is always pleasant or that the pleasure taken in submission surpasses the unhappiness it can create. But the truth that Beauvoir brings to light is as obvious as it sounds scandalous: submission is appealing. Beauvoir describes with an abundance of details "the passive delights"[1] that the girl enjoys in making herself sexual prey, the pleasure that the married woman takes in reigning over her home, and the pleasure that the mother takes in alienating herself to her child.

Beauty

In bringing this pleasure to light, Beauvoir unveils the ambiguity of submission: contrary to what its negative connotation could lead us to think, submission has positive and negative aspects; it is chosen and it is not; it is an abdication before the man and a power over him; it is a source of pleasure and doomed to failure. A good example of these ambiguities is the submission manifested by women's relation to beauty. As Beauvoir shows, beauty does not have the same meaning for men and for women: "The goal of the fashion to which she is enslaved is not to reveal her as an autonomous individual but, on the contrary, to cut her from her transcendence so as to offer her as a prey to male desires."[2] However, this "vocation as a sex object"[3] is not lived by women as negative. On the contrary, women often delight in turning themselves into carnal prey, in touching the soft fabrics in which they drape themselves, and in looking at their beautiful reflection in the mirror. They are pleased to stage and arouse men's desire. Women obtain a pleasurable erotic power over men in making themselves prey.

But this pleasure in submission has its pitfalls: men make women's beauty a manifestation of their power. Beauvoir describes the well-known phenomenon of the trophy woman:

> From one man to another, the festivity takes on the appearance of a potlatch; each of them gives the vision of this body that is his property to all the others as a gift. In her evening dress, the woman is disguised as woman for all the males' pleasure and the pride of her owner.[4]

From Helen of Troy to the models in *Sex and the City*, the same phenomenon repeats itself: men use women's beauty to manifest their power. Everything in women's education entices them to be part of this competition, without grasping the impasse it leads to: in her effort to be a coveted object for men, woman disappears as a subject. Even if she takes pleasure in it, she negates herself at the very moment she believes she is affirming herself: she is not respected or admired for who she is but for her body's physical appearance.

More broadly, seeking to distinguish herself through her physical appearance throws woman into an endless dependency since she needs an external gaze to appreciate what she is, her value, and her identity. If her sense of herself is based only on men's appreciation of her beauty, she will constantly need men's presence in her life, and, more importantly, she may suffer deeply from the changes in her beauty as she ages.

The feminine illusions that structure submission also offer Beauvoir an occasion to make remarks that sound troublingly relevant in the aftermath of the Harvey Weinstein scandal. Commenting on what we would call today the feeling of empowerment created in women by working out, Beauvoir writes:

> Today, more than before, woman knows the joys of shaping her body by sports, gymnastics, swimming, massage, and diets; . . . in working out, she affirms herself as subject; this gives her a kind of liberation from her contingent flesh; but this liberation easily lapses back into dependence. The Hollywood star triumphs over nature: but she finds herself a passive object in the producer's hands.[5]

No matter how much pleasure can be obtained by the transformation of the self into an appealing passive object, the result is that the woman-object needs man and his gaze to exist as a woman, whose body is flesh. If the woman succeeds in her endeavor, men will not see her as a subject but as a prey-object ready to be devoured.

Love-Abdication

To transform oneself into a passive erotic object is one of the modes of female submission. Another, which may be the hardest to avoid, is the temptation of devotion, or abdication even, that arises in the "woman in love." This temptation is the one that preoccupies Beauvoir the most, and her memoirs show it is one that she experienced herself. She thus writes, about her first appointment as a philosophy teacher in Marseilles, far from Sartre: "I hoped it would strengthen me against the temptation I had been dodging for two years now: abdicating. All my life I would keep an uneasy memory of this period, of my fear that I might betray my youthful ideals."[6] More broadly, her memoirs as a whole narrate a Beauvoir who does not fully abdicate—since she becomes a writer and leads an existence of her own—but who considers Sartre superior to her throughout her life. From their first conversations in front of the Medici fountain in the Luxembourg gardens, she submits to what she sees as his evident superiority:

> It was the first time in my life that I was feeling intellectually dominated by someone. . . . I had to admit my defeat: besides, I had realized, in the course of our discussion, that many of my opinions were based only on prejudice, dishonesty, or hastily formed concepts, that my reasoning was at fault and that my ideas were in a muddle.[7]

Beauvoir wrote the *Memoirs of a Dutiful Daughter*—and thus this passage—nine years after *The Second Sex*. One can imagine that she would see the relationship between the abdication of the woman in love that she describes in *The Second Sex* and her own. Yet she does not see in her defeat the consequence of some sort of arrogance on Sartre's part—although she narrates a few pages earlier how Sartre, when he heard she had passed the first step of the *agrégation*, an exam he had failed the year before and was retaking, told her, "From now on, I'm going to take you under my wing."[8] She sees this, or at least presents it to her reader,[9] as a sign of an inferiority that, in her eyes, will last throughout their whole life together. Before Sartre, and despite the reality of their reciprocal influences, she pictures herself throughout her memoirs as his second in command, as the writer when he is a real philosopher, and as merely a commentator when he is a creator. In *The Prime of Life*, she affirms that she chose literature rather than philosophy because of her self-perceived inferiority compared to Sartre.[10] More generally, the current scholarship on the reciprocal influences between Sartre and Beauvoir show that Beauvoir erased all the traces of her philosophical work and of her influence on Sartre from her memoirs, as if she had to preserve the myth of his superiority to her at all costs.[11] Aside from the biographical interest, this aspect of their relationship shows how pervasive this temptation to devotion and submission is: even a famous intellectual woman who was convinced of the importance of her ideas and of her work, who did not get married, and who refused to have children in order to prioritize her career was tempted to devote herself out of love to a man she considered superior to her.

THE SECOND SEX

Beauvoir's account of love is crucial for an analysis of submission because it illustrates that, contrary to the commonly accepted view of submission as sheer passivity, (1) the woman plays an active role in her submission, (2) there is something pleasurable in this submission, and (3) this submission can function as a form of power. Beauvoir's work—her philosophical works, as well as her fiction and her memoirs—provides a description of the woman in love's temptation to abdicate from many points of view and in many situations. A considerable part of *The Second Sex* describes the way in which love takes, in women, the form of abdication, that is, a renouncing of self for the other. The starting point of her phenomenology of love is the following thesis: "The word 'love' has not at all the same meaning for both sexes, and this is a source of the grave misunderstandings that separate them."[12] Men have a conqueror view of love, and love doesn't define their existence,[13] to the extent that even for the most loving men, love's hardships only last for so long and their identity is not engaged in it. On the contrary, for women, love resembles an abdication of the self: female love often consists in "losing herself, body and soul, in the one designated to her as the absolute, as the essential."[14] This is an illustration of Beauvoir's effort, throughout the book, to historicize categories and behaviors in order to counter their supposedly natural character: there is no immutable nature of love, just as there is no immutable nature of femininity. Love is a feeling that is produced by a certain historical, economic, and social situation. It is thus not surprising that the way sexual difference is coded in a society is reflected not only in the definition of love but in the lived experiences of love.

The specificity of women's lived experience, what makes their experience one of oppression, comes from this love-abdication that is presented to girls and then to women as the achievement of their existence as well as a resignation. In addition to its value in describing the destiny of the woman in love in itself, Beauvoir's chapter on the woman in love is crucial to her analysis of female oppression because it contains the most important features of her account of submission. It offers a phenomenology of female submission and highlights its ambiguity—submission is not sheer passivity and can even constitute a form of power—and its inauthenticity.

Love, for women, is a particularly deep form of submission: the woman in love often seeks to dilute herself in the man she loves and to lose her identity in this love she has for him. Transforming the man into a sort of god, she takes pleasure in serving him and gains a sense of herself in renouncing herself. Beauvoir builds on the literary writings of Juliette Drouet, Colette, Mme d'Argoult, Violette Leduc, and many other women but also on the psychoanalyst Helene Deutsch's analyses and her own observations to bring to light this love-submission in which the spontaneous wish is "to be everything for him."[15]

To begin with, love and submission, in their intertwining, deeply define woman's destiny. The young girl learns that her happiness depends on her being loved and that in order to be loved, she needs to make herself prey for a lover: "She learns that to be happy, she has to be loved; to be loved, she has to await love."[16] The formation of the woman makes her aware that her value comes from the outside, that it comes from man's gaze and love. First and foremost, she needs to be chosen, to be loved.

Beauvoir proposes a phenomenology of the forms of this abdication. But what her analysis of love reveals about submission is that, contrary to the commonly held idea of submission as sheer passivity, the woman plays an active role in her submission, sometimes basks in it, and sometimes even draws pleasure and power from it. She writes:

> To *make* oneself object, to *make* oneself passive, is very different from *being* a passive object: a woman in love is neither asleep nor a corpse; there is a surge in her that ceaselessly falls and rises: it is this surge that creates the spell that perpetuates desire.[17]

The ambiguity of submission is here summed up: it is a mistake to think that the submissive destiny of woman is only imposed on her from the outside. On the contrary, as it appears clearly in the character of the woman in love, the woman *acts* in order to conform to social norms established by male domination. Beauvoir highlights the "passive delights" of submission, the source of a troubling mix of pain and pleasure that comes from submission, and which is far from being merely endured passivity.

However, Beauvoir does not limit herself to describing the main features of this abdication; she also shows its impasses and lies. The submissive woman in love is not a victim of the man she loves. First, it is not an individual man nor the nature of sexes that calls for such a love but the situation in which women find themselves. It is because she is "closed off in the sphere of the relative, destined for the male from her earliest childhood, used to seeing him as a sovereign, with whom equality is not permitted"[18] that the woman thinks of love and lives it as a submission. Second, this submission carries in itself its future failure because it is independent from the actual qualities of the loved man: "he cannot justify the woman who devotes herself to worshipping him."[19] To justify her abdication, the woman endows the man she loves with quasi-divine qualities. The contrast between the qualities the chosen man should have to justify the way she gives herself up for him and the reality of his qualities demonstrates the ambiguity of submission: since no human being can equal a god, any woman that submits to a man out of love prepares herself to be disillusioned. Why give up everything for someone who does so little to deserve it?

From this question, Beauvoir then shows how submission can transform itself into a taking up of power and a form of

domination: when the woman, contrary to what she was hop-
ing, doesn't find the justification of her existence in the man,
that is, when the man doesn't seem sufficiently worthy of and
grateful for the sacrifice she thinks she made for him, "her
generosity is immediately converted into demands."[20] This is
the inevitable deadlock of loving submission: "Her joy is to
serve him: but he must gratefully recognize this service; giving becomes demand according to the customary dialectic of
devotion."[21] In making herself a slave, the woman acquires a
form of power over the man: she considers that her sacrifice
gives the man some duties. Out of love, she makes herself his
slave and thus enchains him.

BEAUVOIR, THE NOVELIST OF SUBMISSIVE LOVE

Though this analysis of submission out of love is rendered concrete through her phenomenological method, Beauvoir gives
her portrait of this phenomenon even more depth in multi-
plying perspectives and types of first-person narration of it
throughout her oeuvre. In *The Mandarins*, first published in
1954, Beauvoir develops the character of Paula, a woman in love
who devotes herself fully to Henri, the man she loves, to the
point of suffocating him. In contrast to Anne, the other female
character, who refuses "making a career of being a wife,"[22]
Paula gives herself over to Henri. When he wants to go on a
reporting trip with another woman, she refuses, blackmails
him, and uses her own abdication to prevent him from leav-
ing. She tells him: "I'd take anything from you, anything!" He
responds: "If you decide that you suffer when I do what I want

to, then I'll have to choose between you and my freedom."[23]
Here is the ambiguity of the loving abdication: the woman who
makes a man the whole of her existence finds in her own abdication grounds to enchain him. And in so doing, she puts the man
in such a position that he can only reject this too invasive love
and thus plunge her into the terror of losing what defines her.

The relationship between Paula and Henri manifests the
difference between the male and the female way of loving in a
striking way. Paula recognizes it herself: when Henri ascribes
their disagreement to a misunderstanding on the nature of love,
she responds: "I know what you're going to say—my love is my
whole life and you want it to be only a part of yours. I know,
and I agree."[24] Her abdication is so complete that she claims
her dependency and doesn't seek to avoid it. As the novel continues, Paula's submission to Henri deepens, and with it the
unavoidable rejection it provokes. Beauvoir depicts a Paula
who increasingly abdicates while being entirely aware of the
paradoxes of her submission. She thus tells Henri:

> To want you as I had dreamed of you and not as you are was
> to prefer myself to you. It was pure presumptuousness. But
> that's over. There's only you; I'm nothing. I accept being
> nothing, and I'll accept anything from you. . . . It's my fault;
> I had too much pride. The road of self-abnegation isn't easy,
> you know. But I swear to you now: I'll ask nothing more
> for myself. You alone exist, and you can demand anything
> of me.[25]

Paula's example is unequivocal: loving submission places
woman in a state of dependency and, at the same time, this

submission is much more than mere abdication because of the almost aggressive logic of devotion that gives the person who devotes herself the feeling that her devotion generates duties for the one who receives it. Through her submission, woman unloads on man the burden of finding a meaning for her life. And she seizes a power over man that is almost as important as the power man has over her: the duty to be worth the immense sacrifice that is offered to him.

Whether with Paula in *The Mandarins* or with the female narrator of *The Woman Destroyed*, who is abandoned by her husband and her daughters despite her absolute submission, Beauvoir reveals the ambiguities of submission: far from total and unilateral abdication, submission is a form of devotion that wishes to enchain the other but which, in so doing, dooms itself to failure. The woman in love gives herself fully to the other and in so doing hopes to find a justification for her existence. At the same time, she would like him to be devoted to her as fully as she is devoted to him, which would make both their existences pointless since what gives existence meaning according to Beauvoir is to have projects and to exert one's freedom in the world. The woman in love says she wants to be nothing else than fully devoted to the man she loves, but she enchains him through her need of him. Thus, this love condemns her to waiting and to being abandoned: though love does not harm man's subjectivity and ambition, female love condemns woman to be Penelope waiting for Ulysses at best. At worst, it condemns her to be Dido, abandoned in the middle of the night by Aeneas, whom the gods of Olympus reminded he had better things to do than to lose himself in a woman's love.

The Power of Submission

Through her concept of submission and through her analysis of the body lived as an object, Beauvoir shows that women's choices are limited by male domination. Yet she still considers that women in Western societies have agency. In accordance with the distinction she made in *The Ethics of Ambiguity* between the woman enclosed in a harem and the Western woman, Beauvoir argues that there are different degrees of constraint and, therefore, different degrees of complicity with men: some women are not fully constrained and yet submit themselves. As she wrote then, "We have said that it would be contradictory deliberately to will oneself not free. But one can choose not to will himself free."[26] The problem is thus understanding why women who could choose freedom choose submission.

AN ACTIVE PASSIVITY

These women are not simply dominated by an indiscriminate force attributed to men; *they submit themselves*. They are thus, as the verb form shows, active in this situation that seems to manifest their passivity. Beauvoir claims that "to *make* oneself object, to *make* oneself passive, is very different from *being* a passive object."[27] Submission is an attitude, and as such it is not something that is forced upon the submissive person from the outside but something this person does. This is the case, for instance, with the woman who gets ready before going out, who shaves, puts on shapewear, straightens her hair, and applies makeup in order to turn herself into a beautiful object. She will undoubtedly look like an object, but an object she will have shaped herself.

Beauvoir devotes a whole part of the second volume of *The Second Sex* to what she calls the "justifications" of women: narcissism, love, and mysticism. These are the principal means women use to escape the negative side of their destiny by justifying it. They are "this ultimate effort—sometimes ridiculous, often pathetic—of the imprisoned woman to convert her prison into a heaven of glory, her servitude into sovereign freedom."[28] Through these figures, she shows that there is a form of power in the annihilation of the self.

Though, as we established, Beauvoir rejects the application of the master-slave dialectic to the relations between men and women, she explains women's consent to submission through another dialectic, the one of the servant and the idol. To be clear, it is not a dialectic of the woman's relation to man but of her relation to herself as it is mediated by men's gaze. This dialectic is, for instance, manifest in the married woman:

> Man has only a middling interest in his domestic interior because he has access to the entire universe and because he can affirm himself in his projects. Woman, instead, is locked into the conjugal community: she has to change this prison into a kingdom. Her attitude to her home is dictated by this same dialectic that generally defines her condition: she takes by becoming prey, she liberates herself by abdicating; by renouncing the world, she means to conquer a world.[29]

This dialectic is explained by woman's economic and social situation. For Beauvoir, it is first and foremost a woman's condition of being confined in the home that positions her as inferior. Since woman depends economically and socially on the man, she has no choice: she must get married, she must make herself prey for men. Beauvoir regularly insists on the fact that woman does not submit happily. From the little girl who envies boys who climb trees to the mother who makes sure her daughter will not be more autonomous than she is out of spite for her own condition, women are continuously depicted as both irritated and resigned in the face of this submission that imposes itself on them. Of course, it may seem like women are considerably less economically and socially dependent on men than they were in 1949: at the time, in France, a woman could not have a bank account or a driver's license without her husband's approval. Yet Beauvoir's analyses remain valid. For example, women's financial independence remains an issue: in many parts of the United States, a woman who devoted many years to staying at home to raise her kids, thus allowing her husband to work long hours, will not get properly compensated for the loss of income that occurred from this situation in case of a divorce. But more importantly, the social pressure of heterosexual marriage remains very strong: being a single woman is still stigmatized and, conversely, being a wife continues to be seen in a positive light, as if the fact a man wanted a particular woman enough to marry her is a sign of her value. The social norms surrounding domestic work and motherhood and the gendered way girls and boys are still raised today are good reasons to think that despite the progress made since 1949, the core of Beauvoir's analyses remains valid.

Beauvoir then shows that this dialectical movement, which manifests a possibility for women to "turn their prison into a kingdom," that is, to make themselves subjects in the very heart of their oppression, opens up to them. In conceiving of herself as the queen of the kingdom that is her home, the woman converts her oppression into an omnipotence. In this way, submission is for her an occasion to seize power. This, however, is, according to Beauvoir, an illusion since it consists in transposing to the home the quest of transcendence that drives any human existence, while the housewife existence plunges women in an irreversible immanence. At the same time, woman obtains benefits from it. And this is where Beauvoir's analysis is powerful: it shows that women consent to their submission, but this consent is not vain: it allows woman, in fact, to not purely endure a destiny that is imposed on her.

Submission thus appears in its ambiguity: to woman it seems the only available strategy to get sovereignty, to acquire a form of mastery of the self and the world that is akin to autonomy. Beauvoir insists on this ambiguity, using as examples women's sadomasochistic practices, including the self-mutilation of young girls and what she calls the sadomasochism of mothers. She thus describes the self-mutilation of girls:

> Destined to be a passive prey, she claims her freedom right up to submitting to pain and disgust. When she inflicts the cut of the knife, the burning of a coal on herself, she is protesting against the penetration that deflowers her: she protests by nullifying it. Masochistic, since she welcomes the pain caused by her behavior, she is above all sadistic: as autonomous subject, she beats, scorns, and tortures this dependent flesh, this flesh condemned to submission that she detests but from which she does not want to separate

herself. Because, in all these situations, she does not choose authentically to reject her destiny. Sadomasochistic crazes imply a fundamental bad faith: if the girl indulges in them, it means she accepts, through her rejections, her future as woman; she would not mutilate her flesh with hatred if first she did not recognize herself as flesh. Even her violent outbursts arise from a situation of resignation.[30]

This illustrates the way in which consent to submission works: the girl is in bad faith since she is caught in the crossfire between a destiny she rejects and a desire for this destiny, between the desire to be prey and the refusal to abandon freedom. Moreover, it is a form of bad faith because the girl refuses to confront the massive problem that she faces: the pleasure she takes in (self)objectification, in turning herself into an object.

THE BENEFITS OF SUBMISSION

Beauvoir shows that women are not purely passive victims of oppression; they also reap benefits from it. It is not solely that women delude themselves about their power in order to bear the fact they are not subjects because they are deprived of the quest of transcendence—which can only occur for those in the public world to which they do not have access. There is also a positive pleasure taken in submission.

The chapters on the girl, on sexual initiation, and on erotism analyze the makeup of female eroticism. These sections show that it is structured by a desire of objectification that Beauvoir repeatedly calls "the delights of passivity." Female eroticism is organized by a conceptual triad of submission-object-passivity. For instance, Beauvoir explains that:

> When female sexuality develops, it is penetrated with the religious feeling that woman has devoted to man since childhood. It is true that the little girl experiences a thrill in the confessional and even at the foot of the deserted altar close to what she will later feel in her lover's arms: woman's love is one of the forms of experience in which a consciousness makes itself an object for a being that transcends it; and these are also the passive delights that the young pious girl tastes in the shadows of the church. . . . Everything encourages her to abandon herself in dreams to the arms of men to be transported to a sky of glory. She learns that to be happy, she has to be loved; to be loved, she has to await love.[31]

There is a specificity to the girl's eroticism that makes her dream about being passive and possessed. This eroticism can assuredly be attributed to education and ideology: the girl is taught to conform to an ideal of femininity that is dictated to her. But it also comes from the pleasures and power that women can draw from their objectification:

> Refusing to be the Other, refusing complicity with man, would mean renouncing all the advantages an alliance with the superior caste confers on them. Lord-man will materially protect liege-woman and will be in charge of justifying her existence: along with the economic risk, she eludes the metaphysical risk of a freedom that must invent its goals without help. Indeed, beside every individual's claim to assert themselves as subject—an ethical claim—lies the temptation

to flee freedom and to make himself into a thing: it is a per-
nicious path because the individual, passive, alienated, and
lost, is prey to a foreign will, cut off from his transcendence,
robbed of all worth. But it is an easy path: the anguish and
stress of authentically assumed existence are thus avoided.
The man who sets the woman up as an *Other* will thus find
in her deep complicities. Hence woman makes no claim
for herself as subject because she lacks the concrete means,
because she senses the necessary link connecting her to man
without positing its reciprocity, and because she often wal-
lows in her role as Other.[32]

In refusing to be a subject, and in making oneself an object,
any human being can elude the cost of freedom. But the relations between men and women are setting the problem, in
a way, before the master-slave dialectic: before choosing
whether or not to risk death, one needs to conceive of oneself
as a subject and to want to be recognized as such. If women's
economic and social situation blocks the impetus of their transcendence, there is an individual and chosen pleasure taken in
alterity that explains submission. The social conditioning is still
present—and, in this respect, Beauvoir's thought is resolutely
anti-essentialist—but it endures in women's thought as a sort
of inner colonization.[33]

Beauvoir thus sheds light on the different factors of consent
to submission: the causes of this consent are primarily political, social, and economic, and they result from the structure
of patriarchy. But this consent also originates in the pleasure
taken in submission, which constitutes a specificity of women's
oppression. Because of the "original *Mitsein*" that they share

with men, women's conformity with the expectations of the oppressor is rewarded in a much greater way than in other oppressed groups. Women who submit themselves consent to a destiny that is assigned to them after a sort of cost-benefit analysis in which the delights of submission are seen to outweigh the risks of freedom.

9

Freedom and Submission

Once we become aware, with Beauvoir's help, of the familiar and diverse forms that female submission takes, an enigma subsists: *Why* do women submit themselves? Looking at the woman in love, the Hollywood star, the satisfied housewife, or the wife of the academic who does his archival work, many of them look neither unhappy nor coerced and some of them take pleasure in their situation. Does this mean that they *choose* their submission? Such a hypothesis seems untenable, if only because these women do not describe their choices as submission; nor do they describe their submission as a choice. We thus go back to the theoretical problem of submission identified at the beginning of the book: either it is a choice, or it is submission. To choose to submit seems impossible or confined to some perverts and masochists: submission can only be justified as a last resort, as for the warrior who must submit or die. How, then, should we understand the tension between our almost instinctive condemnation of submission and its ordinary and daily character? How can we understand, in particular, the fact that there seems to be a typically feminine submission? Does it mean that women are more immoral than men? Or that, for women, this submission is not immoral?

An Ethics of Freedom

THE CORE QUESTION: IS SUBMITTING IMMORAL?

As explained at the beginning of the book, the spontaneous, intuitive reaction to submission is rejection: submission appears as a moral vice against which we hope to guard ourselves. Except for very specific circumstances, like BDSM sex play, no one claims to be submissive. This strong reaction, which manifests the negativity associated with submission, stands in the way of comprehending submission, especially among women. It leads one to instinctively refuse to see in oneself the least submissive behavior and to only identify submission in people we condemn or who seem drastically different from us.

In comparing the figure of the defeated warrior, who dies unless he submits, and the submissive woman, we have noted that the woman functions as the paradigm of a chosen submission. The warrior does not choose his submission, but the woman does, and this choice seems incomprehensible unless a submissive nature of women is posited. There are two possibilities, then: woman is submissive by nature or woman is submissive by choice. But this choice, insofar as it is a free one, seems inexplicable: if I am free to choose, why would I choose to not be free?

Submission as an everyday attitude has not provoked philosophical analysis in the history of philosophy. Some political philosophers, however, have taken up the question of submission of people to ruler(s). Calling it the problem of political obligation, these philosophers have raised the following issues: How can individuals' obedience to the king or to laws be explained? How does this obedience function? Is this obedience a submission? If so, is it contrary to the freedom of the subjects? In the context of this line of questioning, La Boétie and Rousseau have sealed the fate of voluntary servitude: men are naturally and originally free and, because of this nature, to choose to submit is a moral vice because it means renouncing human nature.

Against this idea, in *The Second Sex*, Beauvoir appropriates Sartre's existentialism in a way that allows her to overcome this impasse and to show that it is not a moral inferiority that leads women to consent to their submission. As we noted, the phenomenological method allows Beauvoir to describe submission. Nonetheless, this method does not suffice to explain why women accept submission or to account for what Beauvoir calls "the delights of passivity." We will thus argue that it is by combining the phenomenological method with an existentialist philosophy of freedom that Beauvoir manages to make the choice of submission understandable, as well as shed light on the reasons why it is more a consent than a proper choice.

AN EXISTENTIALIST PERSPECTIVE

In order to fully understand how she responds to the problem of submission, we need to understand what Beauvoir's ethical theory is, which means, in her case, what her existentialism is.

Beauvoir announces in the introduction that she is adopting what she calls "the perspective . . . of existentialist ethics."[1] This wording matters: contrary to the commonly held prejudice that *The Second Sex* is only an application of Sartrean philosophy, Beauvoir shows here that she does not consider existentialism as a philosophical system or as a dogma. While Sartre built an existentialist *ontology* in *Being and Nothingness*, Beauvoir transposes existentialism in the *ethical* sphere and uses it as a "perspective," that is, not as a dogma or a set of solutions but as a way to look at issues.

Philosopher and commentator extraordinaire Michèle Le Dœuff argues that Beauvoir completely alters Sartrean existentialism to the extent that she changes its meaning and its usefulness: with Beauvoir, existentialism becomes a theory that can address social and political issues. Le Dœuff explains that *Being and Nothingness* is structured by an androcentrism[2] (androcentric theories depict the world and establish norms based on men's perspectives, interests, and values) and that this androcentrism borders on sexism.[3] And Sartre's existentialist system makes it impossible to conceptualize oppression, and more broadly the social world, because of the focus on the individual and his relationship to freedom.[4] It thus seems at first glance impossible to use existentialism to analyze and critique women's oppression because Sartre's systematic and individualistic take on existentialism does not allow it. Beauvoir, however, transforms existentialism in such a way that it becomes politically powerful. *The Second Sex* is therefore not an application of Sartre's philosophy but an original philosophical work that redefines existentialism.

When she mentions the existentialist "perspective," Beauvoir refers to a certain ethical position, inherited from Kierkegaard, which consists in starting from the individual, her existence, and her first-person experience in order to understand humankind. Against a philosophical tendency to seek universal abstract truths about humankind, the existentialist perspective starts from the individual, from what is singular in each human existence. This commitment to approach the universal only from the singular was already at the root of the phenomenological method, and it is crucial in Beauvoir's conceptualization of freedom.

The existentialist ethics perspective has several consequences for Beauvoir. First at stake is the adoption of an individual perspective. This does not mean that Beauvoir advocates for a methodological atomism or individualism, in that she would consider that the individual precedes the social or that the social would solely be the sum of individuals. The individual perspective she chooses consists simply in grounding normative judgments on the good of the individual rather than the good of society. As she writes it, "We judge institutions from the point of view of the concrete opportunities they give to individuals."[5]

Second, this individual perspective does not mean that the only thing that matters is the subjective happiness of individuals:

Are women in a harem not happier than a woman voter? Is a housewife not happier than a woman worker? We do not really know what the word "happiness" means, and still less

> what authentic values it covers; there is no way to measure
> the happiness of others, and it is always easy to call a situ-
> ation that one would like to impose on others happy: in
> particular, we declare happy those condemned to stagna-
> tion, under the pretext that happiness is immobility.[6]

Beauvoir's precision here is important for us: women's well-
being is one of the commonly used arguments in support of
gender inequalities; women are submissive because it makes
them happy. Indeed, submission can be a source of pleasure for
women; one of the strengths of *The Second Sex* is its demonstra-
tion of this. But it would be dangerous to conclude from this
pleasure that submission would be *good* for women.

This distinction can be better understood through an
anachronistic detour. One of the commonly held theories of
economics and rational choice theory is the idea that choices
reveal preferences. Economist and philosopher Amartya Sen
has shown that individuals adapt their preferences and the
evaluation of their well-being to the situation in which they
find themselves.[7] In particular, Sen shows that adapting one's
preferences to fit the situation one finds oneself in is a rational
protection mechanism for individuals who find themselves in
situations of extreme deprivation. Adapting their preferences
allows them to not add to their suffering the pain of lamenting about it. Sen uses the example of extremely poor women
from rural India who have almost no access to food because the
meager resources of their family go primarily to their husband
and children. Sen finds that these women are convinced that
they have very limited, if not nonexistent, nutritional needs,
that they need much less than their husbands and children.

Sen shows that this belief stems from the fact that there is no available food and thus believing one does not need food is a rational way to deal with the situation. This example manifests that individuals have adaptive preferences and adapt to the situation they find themselves in, including when such an adaptation is objectively harmful for them. Similarly, there are cases of submission that are objectively harmful for women and that could still be described as a perfectly bearable, if not happy, situation.

Sen uses this observation to emphasize a serious shortfall of classical economics (which posits that welfare is the primary criterion of value): welfare economics can go against social justice.[8] Welfare economics indeed considers welfare as subjective and accomplished—as the welfare that individuals currently estimate they enjoy. But such a subjective measurement could lead people who have almost nothing but have adapted their preferences to their situation to appear as well-off or even better-off than people who are objectively in a good situation but are unhappy about their lot. Focusing only on maximizing welfare as it is defined by welfare economics can therefore lead to tremendous social injustice. We thus understand how there is no necessary contradiction between the negative character of submission and an apparent subjective happiness of the person who submits: it is likely[9] that male domination leads women to adapt their preferences in such a way that they end up happy with their situation, even though this situation is objectively harmful for them.

In refusing to ground her ethics on subjective evaluations of happiness, Beauvoir avoids the pitfall underlined by Sen. Beauvoir's adoption of a perspective centered on the individual does not imply a subjective conception of the good. Beauvoir clarifies what the existentialist perspective is: it is a concrete humanism.

Finally, in the existentialist perspective there is no abstract or objective response to the question of knowing what a woman is. It is only through individual experiences that this question finds a response. This existentialist claim thus grounds the structure of the book as well as the use of phenomenology in the second volume: to seek general answers from the individual entails to wonder what a woman is from men's and from women's point of view, but also what is the experience that men and women have of what is called femininity.

In sum, the existentialist perspective that Beauvoir adopts focuses on the individual rather than society as a whole, rejects a subjective understanding of well-being in favor of a concrete humanism in which freedom is the core value, and proceeds from singular experiences and not from abstract theories about humanity.

FREEDOM IS A CONQUEST

This existentialist perspective structures Beauvoir's conception of freedom. When she claims to adopt the perspective of existentialist ethics, she is referring to the existentialist theory of freedom. The central thesis of existentialism is that the human being is a freedom: what we are, our essential characteristic, is this freedom, which is why our existence precedes our essence. Because we are essentially free, we are essentially free to determine what we are (our essence) through the way we live this freedom (our existence). Different from a paper cutter, for instance, whose essence is predetermined by its function (cutting paper), there is no predetermined essence of human beings; each human being shapes her existence through her freedom.

Yet freedom is not merely a quality of human beings; it requires an active engagement in the world. Freedom must be exerted in the sense that humans must engage with the world and manifest their freedom through projects. From the description of human nature as free, existentialism draws normative conclusions: one *ought to* live according to this freedom. This means that the human being must recognize herself as free and must act freely. One should not take refuge behind some determinism to justify one's actions but recognize oneself as the subject of each of one's actions. (This type of attitude is precisely what Sartre calls bad faith.) For instance, it is wrong to pretend one acts out of obligation or out of duty while one always freely chooses to respect or not one's duties and obligations.

Because of this absolute freedom, existentialist ethics cannot be made of prescriptions or rules, except the rule of living in an authentically free way. Indeed, moral rules are by definition in opposition to humans' exercise of absolute freedom: authentically living according to our absolute freedom is recognizing that we are the instance who determines what is right or wrong. As Beauvoir writes in "Existentialism and Popular Wisdom": "Man may not be naturally good, but he is not naturally bad either; he is nothing at first. It is up to him to make himself good or bad depending on whether he assumes his freedom or renounces it."[10]

This prescription emphasizes that freedom is double-edged: on the one hand, there is something exhilarating in knowing oneself to be free. On the other hand, to be the only master of one's existence is distressing. Risk and uncertainty are at the heart of freedom: freedom is not a given; it is something for the subject to conquer. Freedom is not static; it expresses itself through projects. It is a transcendence in the sense that it consists in going toward indetermination. To be free is to project oneself onto the world. Therefore, freedom comprises risks; it demands the courage and the self-confidence that are necessary to determine a project for oneself and to throw oneself into an undetermined world in which the success of the project is not guaranteed.

Beauvoir sheds light on this cost in *Ethics of Ambiguity* through a phenomenological description of the genealogy of the ethical subject,[11] that is, on the different stages of ethical development throughout life. The individual is born into a world in which values, authorities, and meanings are already established. In that respect, the child depends on the world and has to conform to it. Being a child is being a being who cannot yet exert its absolute freedom and autonomously decide for itself what is the right and the wrong way to be free. Growing up, the teenager learns to project herself into the world and progressively frees herself from her dependency. But this freedom has a cost due to the risks the subject exposes herself to in pursuing it. Teenagers oftentimes experience anguish in the face of their freedom to choose and the price they could have to pay for their decisions (e.g., if a teenager decides to skip school, she may be punished by her parents or by a school administrator). The cost of freedom can be significant enough that it creates a desire in the teenager or adult to go back to their situation as a child, where obedience and dependency meant avoiding the existential anguish of freedom. What this genealogy shows is that freedom is ambiguous: it is the source of morality and of existential flourishing, and at the same time it is inseparable from existential anguish.

Why Women Submit to Men

THE SOLUTION OF THE THEORETICAL PROBLEM OF SUBMISSION

This conception of freedom as both an urge felt by everyone and a costly risk is the last element we need to respond to the problem of female submission. Indeed, it shows that (1) submission is not a relinquishing of a freedom one already has but a renouncement to pursue freedom, and (2) a renouncement to pursue freedom is tempting for all human beings, but (3) women's situation makes freedom more costly and thus submission is more appealing to women than men. Therefore (4) it is not that women actively choose submission but that they consent to the submission that is prescribed to them by social norms.

This theory of freedom is crucial and dissolves the apparent antinomy of consent to submission. As we saw at the beginning of the book, in classical political philosophy, especially in Rousseau's work, it is impossible to voluntarily submit because this submission is a relinquishing of freedom. The starting hypothesis is that men are born free, that is to say, that any situation that is not freedom must come from the transformation of an initial freedom. Submission can then only be explained as an alienation of freedom—as a renouncement of freedom. And no rational mind should want to alienate their freedom. Therefore, no one should consent to submission.

On the contrary, in the genealogy proposed by Beauvoir, submission is the first condition of the individual.[12] While it is true that humans' nature is their freedom, this freedom is a potentiality, not an actuality. The individual is first a baby, then a child—submissive beings in the sense that they do what their parents and educators decide for them—and they must act in order to emerge from this first state of submission. Becoming free, for the teenager, implies acting. Freedom is a costly movement in order to extract oneself from one's facticity.

In this understanding of freedom as requiring concrete actions, there is no contradiction in the idea of consenting to submission. Submission can be seen as the decision to stay in a childlike situation, that is to say, to not actively pursue freedom. If freedom only happens when one actively projects oneself onto the world, then submission is not, as in Rousseau's view, an active decision to renounce freedom; it can be a passive attitude of not actively pursuing freedom.

This is very important because it makes submission less mysterious: it is harder to understand why someone who is free would suddenly decide to give up this freedom and submit herself than to understand why someone would not make the active decision to act freely. To give a concrete example, submission can look like the decision someone might make to go to medical school when they are not particularly attracted to it but that's what is expected in their family of doctors instead of trying to figure out what they would really like to do with their life. Such a decision is not an active renouncement to be free; it is a passive acceptance of the way that is paved for oneself.

There is, therefore, no longer a contradiction in the very idea of a choice or a consent to submission, yet a problem remains: If humans are free and if acting ethically consists in acting freely, why would some people prefer submission to freedom?

SUBMISSION IS A GENERAL TEMPTATION

Existentialism recognizes the anguish that all human beings feel in the face of freedom, as well as the temptation to abdicate that springs from it. Sartre only considers this problem of abdication from an individual angle. For him, the struggle between freedom and renunciation happens between the individual and himself. The problem of such an approach, in Beauvoir's view, as we explained earlier, is that it ignores the ways in which social structures influence this struggle. Beauvoir thus complicates and transforms the existentialist analysis of freedom thanks to her concept of situation: yes, everyone is tempted by abdication and renunciation to freedom, yet the strength of this temptation depends on the situation in which individuals find themselves.

From *The Ethics of Ambiguity* on, Beauvoir distinguishes between two cases: one in which the individual's situation is such that they cannot project themselves toward freedom[13] and one in which the individual chooses to not be free in order to benefit from the privileges of submission:

It is then that we discover the difference which distinguishes them from an actual child: the child's situation is imposed upon him, whereas the woman (I mean the western woman of today) chooses it or at least consents to it. Ignorance and error are facts as inescapable as prison walls. The Black slave of the eighteenth century, the Muslim woman enclosed in a harem have no instrument, be it in thought or by astonishment or anger, which permits them to attack the civilization which oppresses them. Their behavior is defined and can be judged only within this given situation, and it is possible that in this situation, limited like every human situation, they realize a perfect assertion of their freedom. But once there appears a possibility of liberation, it is resignation of freedom to not exploit the possibility, a resignation which implies bad faith and which is a positive fault.[14]

Beauvoir draws a clear distinction between forced submission, in which agency almost completely disappears and for which, therefore, the individual cannot be held accountable, and complicit submission—the submission that comes from the temptation of sparing oneself the cost of freedom and taking advantage of the benefits of submission. In that case, there is, in Beauvoir's view, moral fault.

Thus there is a temptation of submission that is inherent to the human condition and to the necessity of acting in order to be free. Nonetheless, explaining women's submission in that way, ascribing it to the cost of freedom, seems to refute the hypothesis of a specificity of female submission: all human beings are likely to try to escape existential anguish through the bad faith consisting in pretending nothing can be done to free oneself. There seems to be no reason to think women would act more in bad faith than would men.

SUBMISSION IS MORE TEMPTING FOR WOMEN

In fact, women do have a characteristic that makes them more likely to be in bad faith, but it has nothing to do with a hypothetical feminine essence. Women are more likely to submit than men because of their situation. As Beauvoir explains in *The Ethics of Ambiguity*:

> Certain adults can live in good faith: those who are denied all instruments of escape, those who are enslaved or who are mystified. The less economic and social circumstances allow an individual to act upon the world, the more this world appears to him as given. This is the case of women who inherit a long tradition of submission.[15]

This passage is crucial in many ways. First, it demonstrates Beauvoir's originality in an existentialist tradition that never considers the economic, social, and political dimensions of the concrete character of existence. Second, it shows that there are, according to Beauvoir, degrees of bad faith, degrees of freedom, depending on the economic and social situations of individuals. Therefore, Beauvoir conceives of the possibility of a submission that is not a form of bad faith: depending on the degree of social and economic enslavement of the woman, her submission could even be a sign of good faith. In any case, the very fact that male domination has economic and social consequences that reduce women's freedom entails that her submission is not pure bad faith.

The consequence of Beauvoir's conception of situated freedom is crucial for our analysis of submission: if all human beings are beset by the dilemma between submission and freedom, women are much more affected by this dilemma because of their situation and of the tradition of submission they inherit. This situation is a product of the gendered upbringing that Beauvoir meticulously describes in the "Formation" part of the second volume. Girls learn to conceive of themselves not only as weak and fragile but as weaker and more fragile than boys. During their upbringing, they are constantly compared to boys, resulting in the perception of themselves as the inessential and weak Other. But this situation is first and foremost the result of the control men have over the definition of the female subject. And this explains Beauvoir's decision, surprising at first glance, to study men's views on women before analyzing women's lived experiences. Through this organization of her book, Beauvoir emphasizes that the most important component of women's situation is that it is conceived, built, and imposed from the outside, by men who see them as the Other and, therefore, as destined to inferiority. The second volume must thus be read as the phenomenology of the impact on women of the facts and myths of the first volume.

This constitution from the outside explains, for instance, one of the most problematic traits of women's lives for whoever would want to emancipate them: unlike Jews, Blacks, or workers, women do not (or, at least, did not until very recently) perceive themselves as belonging to an oppressed *group*. They conceive of themselves as united to men much more than united to each other. This "original *Mitsein*" that exists between men and heterosexual women makes male domination more discrete and female submission more likely.

Combining the perspective of existentialist ethics, the original theory of freedom that structures it, and the concept of situation, Beauvoir opens the possibility of understanding female submission as the result of a cost-benefit analysis.[16] Like men, women are torn between the desire and the anguish of freedom, between the will to project themselves onto the world and the temptation to abdicate. Unlike men, however, submission is socially prescribed to women. There are therefore possible advantages for them in submitting. For instance, the slim young woman, who has shaped her body through diets and workouts, who is pretty, well made-up, and gives men the attention they think they deserve, will be the object of men's attentions, while the independent woman risks being lonely or rejected from a society in which heterosexual marriage remains the norm if she does not play the game of femininity. In the patriarchal context, woman's situation thus alters the equilibrium between costs and benefits of freedom and makes freedom much more costly for women than for men. This is true to the extent that even the most ambitious women sometimes prefer renouncing their freedom rather than paying the (high) price for it—for instance, taking up most of the housework to avoid the catastrophic economic consequences of a divorce or ensuring that the husband does not feel humiliated by his wife's higher salary.[17]

A CONSENT THAT IS NOT A CHOICE

If submission is the result of a cost-benefit analysis that is tilted toward submission by the patriarchal social norms, then it is a mistake to understand submission as a choice. Submission is a consent to one's destiny as it is predetermined by social norms. The freedom at stake in classical political philosophy is not the same as the freedom of choice in daily life. The freedom that Rousseau had in mind when he claimed that no one can alienate it without losing their humanity is an abstract right that all individuals possess by the very fact of being human. Whereas the freedom that is manifested in the choice of submitting is an anthropological given, a quality of the human being, that is also called agency—or the ability to act. Though the political conception of freedom is crucial in evaluating the organization of society, it produces mostly ideal and normative theories. For those who seek to understand, in a concrete and non-ideal way,[18] how power relations between individuals structure themselves, such a conception of freedom cannot provide tools for fighting injustice.

By building a concrete theory of freedom, in which freedom appears as a universally shared drive but with unequally distributed costs, Beauvoir highlights the specific attraction of submission for women. Humans have in common an ambiguous relation to freedom: if freedom is not given, it means it must be conquered, and such a conquest carries risks, primarily the risk of failure. Humans are tempted to turn their backs on transcendence in order to keep the soothing pleasures of immanence, of a predictable and submissive existence. Yet there is a specificity to women's submission. Even if they desire their freedom, even if they have the same taste for the absolute as the most adventurous of men, they know that because of the structure of male domination, seeking freedom comes at an excessively higher cost for them than for men. This is still true in the twenty-first century: a woman who travels on her own is at greater risk of being sexually attacked than a man; a woman who refuses to have children because she values other experiences more than parenthood will be judged in a considerably harsher way than a man; a mother who does not attend her children's school events because of the time constraints and responsibilities of her career will often be perceived as a bad mother when a father would not; a female manager will often be perceived as bossy and angry when her male counterpart would be seen as efficient when displaying the same behaviors; women's physical appearance is held against them professionally;[19] and the way butch lesbians are discriminated against illustrates the cost, for women, of not playing by the rules of mainstream femininity. And, conversely, there are many rewards to be had in submission. A slim, good-looking woman may be able to get out of a traffic ticket, she may be served faster in a bar, or she may get a job because of her good looks; a woman who does all the housework in her home will be praised as a good homemaker; a woman who constantly volunteers at school events will be seen as a good mother; and a woman who does as she is told by her community will be praised for being a good daughter to her parents. Women have structural reasons to agree to submit.

In this context of the cost-benefit analysis of freedom, a crucial issue is that for women, the costs of freedom are easier to measure than its benefits. Indeed, the social norms and their enforcement mechanisms appear quite clearly and can be measured through quantitative studies whereas the main benefits of freedom, and the main costs of unfreedom, are harder to quantify. An instantiation of this idea can be found in the case study by philosopher Ann Cudd:[20] she proposes a simple rational choice case involving a couple, Larry and Lisa, who are exactly similar in terms of age, talent, education, and professional experience, who do not hold sexist conceptions on the division of labor, and who decide to have a child. She shows that the social structure, and especially gender stereotypes and the gender wage gap, are such that Lisa will decide to stay at home and raise the child, while Larry will work outside the home. This decision is rational given the costs of childcare, the social norms, and the gender gap. However, such a choice will put Lisa in a situation of vulnerability and strategic weakness toward Larry: Will she be able to leave him if he turns out to be violent? What will happen to her and her income if he leaves her? There are good reasons to think, for instance, that Lisa will be more likely to accept things from Larry because she will know that a separation would be catastrophic for her. This last part of the costs of submission is harder to factor in the decision—if only because young married couples have a tendency to think they will love each other forever. More generally, it is harder to evaluate how much we will gain living a free life and how costly unfreedom will be because the costs and the benefits are not necessarily tangible—how can we measure the satisfaction of living the life we want to live?—and may change over time. What Beauvoir's existentialism teaches us is that the benefits of freedom and the costs of unfreedom are the most important costs and benefits, yet they are the least likely to be taken into account in the cost-benefit analysis of submission. This explains why women often decide to submit on the ground of the structural incentives to submission without being able to evaluate how harmful this decision may be to them.

This is why women's decision to submit is not, strictly speaking, a choice. In the context of Beauvoir's philosophy as one centered on the individual and her freedom, to choose is to decide to use one's freedom, to throw oneself onto the world. Conversely, the submissive woman is the woman who, passive about her life, does not seek to conquer a freedom of any sort against her situation—the submission to which she is destined. Submission is a destiny that is always already there for woman; therefore, to submit consists mainly in doing nothing to oppose this destiny, in letting social norms, and the men who define these social norms, decide for her. Most of the time, woman does not actively choose her submission; she merely accepts what is suggested to her. She consents to her destiny of a submissive woman.

Toward Emancipation

This assessment should not drive us to despair—quite the contrary. The analysis of women's submission serves an emancipatory project. Like Beauvoir, we are not shedding light on this consent to submission in order to blame women or, simply, to emphasize the darkness of their condition. Beauvoir describes in all these figures of submissive woman forms of resistance or disgust for submission.[21] And she continually stresses that this submission is obtained by men against the freedom that women aspire to as human beings. When Beauvoir understands the human condition as naturally ambiguous and as depending on a situation that is historically, socially, and economically determined, she opens up possibilities of emancipation. And the millions of women who saw in *The Second Sex* the sign and the manifestation of an emancipation to come made no mistake about it.

SUBMISSION IS NOT INEVITABLE

From the analysis of consent to submission, *The Second Sex* produces a path to emancipation on several levels. In unveiling the way in which women's situation results from historical, religious, theoretical, and mythical constructions made by men instead of a submissive nature of women, Beauvoir frees submissive women from being accused of bad faith and weakness—an accusation that usually contributes to reinforcing women's oppression.

In showing how and why women consent to their submission, she defuses the use of this consent as a way to assign complete responsibility for this submission to women. Yes, women, insofar as they are human beings and thus can choose their freedom, are responsible for not choosing it; but the way in which their situation is determined from the outside by male domination to the extent that submission is made their destiny is such that they cannot be held liable for this submission. Yes, there is an individual pleasure, which can be chosen to a certain extent, in being the Other and in avoiding the existential anguish of the free subject. But the social and economic structures make the movement toward transcendence more costly for women than for men.

Not only does Beauvoir defuse any attempt to attribute to women complete moral responsibility for their submission, she also shows that this submission is not an inexorable destiny. She historicizes women's submission and thus renders it possible to imagine escaping what has been built by male domination as an inflexible destiny:

As Merleau-Ponty rightly said, man is not a natural species: he is a historical idea. Woman is not a fixed reality but a becoming; it is in her becoming that she has to be compared with man; that is, her *possibilities* should be defined: what skews so many issues is that she is being reduced to what she was, to what she is today, while the question concerns her capacities; the fact is that her capacities manifest themselves clearly only when they have been realized: but the fact is also that when one considers a being who is transcendence and surpassing, it is never possible to close the books.[22]

Once it is understood that woman is, just like man, a becoming, a historical being, and not an Other whose alterity and inferiority would be natural, the fact that submission is a historical attitude and not a fixed one becomes evident. It is because of specific economic, social, and political conditions that women consent to their submission; therefore, this submission could come to an end.

Without a doubt, if a caste is maintained in an inferior position, it remains inferior: but freedom can break the circle; let Blacks vote and they become worthy of the vote; give woman responsibilities and she knows how to assume them; the fact is, one would not think of expecting gratuitous generosity from oppressors; but the revolt of the oppressed at times and changes in the privileged caste at other times create new situations; and this is how men, in their own interest, have been led to partially emancipate women: women need only pursue their rise, and the success they obtain encourages them; it seems most certain that they will sooner or later attain perfect economic and social equality, which will bring about an inner metamorphosis.[23]

Submission, in sum, is the fruit of the situation. Such a claim is crucial because it makes intelligible that submission could be lived as a destiny without truly *being* a destiny. Woman is not destined to submission by her nature, but by a certain social state that is historically situated and economically and politically built. Even if there is a circular relationship between society and individuals that invites one to consider the possibility of social change with pessimism, the existentialist perspective grounded on the individual and his freedom raises the possibility of obstructing the mechanisms that reproduce women's oppression. In taking the risk of freedom, in working outside the home, women can change the social and economic conditions to the point that submission would not appear as their default destiny. In overcoming the dichotomy between individual and structure that prevented a full understanding of submission, Beauvoir historicizes submission and thus makes it possible to oppose it.

MEN ARE NOT (ALL) GUILTY

To say that submission is the fruit of the situation is not only emancipatory insofar as we thus understand that changing the situation could allow an escape from submission. It is also emancipatory because it enables us to clarify the responsibilities of individuals. Through the concept of "situation," Beauvoir shows that women do not bear full responsibility for their consent to submission. But she also shows that *men*, as individuals, are not fully responsible for it either. Individual men are sometimes not doing anything to put women in submissive positions; like women, they are thrown into a world in which there are always already meanings and social norms. In that regard, Beauvoir does not hold individual men responsible when they don't actively participate in perpetuating women's oppression. She only emphasizes that they enjoy, often without realizing it, the privileges of the dominant, which consists in seeing their perspective as the neutral, objective, and thus true one and naturalizing others' alterity.

Beauvoir therefore participates in the construction of an emancipatory path in building a theory of privilege. As the philosopher Sonia Kruks has shown,[24] *The Second Sex* is the first step in Beauvoir's thoughts on the way in which privileged people—and herself in the first place—can think about their own situation. These thoughts will be developed in more detail in her later works, but they already appear in *The Second Sex* regarding men's moral responsibility. If women are constrained by their situation, so are men: Beauvoir shows that while a colonial administrator can cease to be one, a man cannot: "So here he is, thus guilty in spite of himself and oppressed by this fault that he has not committed himself."[25]

Emphasizing the way in which male domination saps even men's freedom, Beauvoir paves the way toward a cooperation between men and women in order to fight patriarchy. Though she takes into account that men are worried that they have a lot to lose in considering woman not as the Other but as a "companion,"[26] she praises the merits of a "brotherhood"[27] between men and women. Here's the last sentence of the book:

> It is within the given world that it is up to man to make the reign of freedom triumph; to carry off this supreme victory, men and women must, among other things and beyond their natural differentiations, unequivocally affirm their brotherhood.[28]

The concept of "situation" allows Beauvoir to bring light to the possibility of a conquest of the original *Mitsein* through brotherhood. The conflict of consciousnesses and the alterity that comes from it are not inevitable: when we understand that the meaning of sex difference is a historical social norm, and therefore can be changed, we open up the possibility of a harmonious relationship between men and women, that between two fraternal freedoms.

HERSELF AS AN EXAMPLE

Finally, by the very fact of writing *The Second Sex*, Beauvoir participates in paving a path to emancipation. Her writing such a book appears as a way to counter the gendered dimension of the dichotomy Subject/Other. As an author, she manifests, by the act of writing and of projecting herself in an oeuvre, that women are not excluded from the quest of transcendence. She embodies the fact that women are not destined to only be the companion of creative men. She indeed emphasizes, in the chapter devoted to the married woman, the mistake made by women who think that when they participate in their husband's project—in helping him or advising him—they realize a personal work or they are free beings:

> In any action, any work, what counts is the moment of choice and decision. The wife generally plays the role of the crystal ball that clairvoyants use: another would do just as well. And the proof is that often the man welcomes another adviser, another collaborator, with the same confidence. Sophia Tolstoy copied her husband's manuscripts and put them in order: he later gave the job to one of his daughters; she understood that even her zeal had not made her indispensable. Only autonomous work can assure the wife an authentic autonomy.[29]

In writing *The Second Sex*, Beauvoir manifests the possibility for a woman to throw herself into such an ambitious project, in this autonomous work that guarantees freedom. In that regard, she breaks the vicious circle of women's oppression.

Conclusion

WHAT NOW?

Submission is neither in women's nature nor their final destiny. Yet patriarchy, like all structures of social domination, creates mechanisms to perpetuate itself, and women's submission is one of them. Femininity is presented as a desirable norm, submission is depicted as a source of pleasure and power, and the dangers of women's freedom are constantly emphasized. Women's submission is complex: it happens on the individual level while being influenced by social structure. It is often a submission to a particular man, but it is primarily a submission to a set of social norms. It can be pleasurable while leading to desperate deadlocks.

This was Simone de Beauvoir's assessment in 1949. Although women's condition has improved and the forms of female submission have evolved since then, women are still in a situation in which submission appears as a destiny to which it is easier to consent than to resist. Recognizing this should not be a reason to despair: recognizing the forms and appeals of submission in ourselves is no doubt an important step on the path to emancipation.

One thing is certain: claiming that submission is not a moral vice but a destiny that women are constantly reminded of incites us to see the problems of consent in a new light, especially in the sexual realm. Indeed, if men and women think that not only must women submit to men but actually like doing so, and that women are prey over which men-hunters must triumph, the structure of love and sex relationships may well be far from the image of two equal partners, with equally considered desires, that is conveyed by the concept of consent. This concept, in its polysemy, suggests that three different levels of reflection on sexual consent must be identified.

First, there is a legal issue of sexual consent: How can we ensure that cases of rape, sexual assault, and sexual harassment be effectively punished under the law? How can we put an end to the dreadful situation described by these figures: in the United States, out of 1,000 sexual assaults, 230 are reported to the police, 46 reports lead to arrest, and only 5 cases will lead to a felony conviction?[1] In sum, how can we ensure that the legal norm of consent—understood as choosing or accepting a proposal—is respected? There are two pitfalls here: the first, and most evident, one is that in the sexual realm only the people involved know what was said and what was done, and therefore it is sometimes difficult for courts to establish the facts. But there is a second pitfall, which may be slowly changing: the presumption that women lie. Be it the way in which Anita Hill and Christine Blasey Ford were treated,[2] or the recurrent insinuation that women could be falsely accusing men to make themselves famous,[3] it is clear that women's reports of abuse are automatically doubted when they publicly claim they did not consent. And this doubt has to do with the norm according to which women should submit to men: in a way, to complain about men's sexual violence is a deviation from the norm of femininity.

The second issue raised by consent is a moral one: How can we conceive of an eroticism that would not be based on the traditional idea that men offer and women consent, which is inegalitarian and sexist? Affirmative consent, that is, the idea that only a verbal and enthusiastic "yes" can mean consent, seems to be the best solution. But in France even more than in the United States, some people wonder if such a norm would not destroy a part of eroticism, which may be violent and unequal in its very nature. However, there is no more a nature of love and eroticism than there is a violent nature of man or a submissive nature of woman. That some people desire to be dominant, others languorous, is no one's concern, but in order for sex to be as minimally oppressive as possible, these positions must be the result of a true choice of all parties involved. And it seems hard to believe that whispering one's desire in the ear of one's lover would necessarily be a turn-off.

Finally, there is a political issue of consent in the context of a patriarchal society like ours, and this is the problem that submission helps us think through. In such a society, men and women grow up in a world organized by gendered social norms that prescribe independence and courage to men, and care and submission to women. It is thus not surprising that some women have a hard time saying "no" to men or that some men have a sense of entitlement to women's care and sexual services. It is now clear that one of the great enemies of an equal concord between men, women, and all the people who do not identify with this binarity is women's consent to their own submission.

NOTES

Preface

1. The phrase "Me Too" was created by the civil rights activist Tarana Burke, who started using it on social media in 2006, but #MeToo became popular as a hashtag after the Harvey Weinstein sexual abuse allegations went public.

2. In France, #MeToo led immediately to another hashtag—#BalanceTonPorc—that literally means "Rat on your pig" and invited women to share not only their story but the name of their attacker. A few days later, a hundred women, including the famous actress Catherine Deneuve and the provocative writer Catherine Millet, wrote an op-ed in *Le Monde* claiming for men a "right to bother" that amounts to a freedom to sexually harass and arguing that women might actually enjoy or at least not mind unwanted sexual physical contact in public transportation.

Chapter 1. Submission: A Philosophical Taboo

1. *The Sexual Life of Catherine M.* is a book in which Catherine Millet, probably the most prominent contemporary art critic in France, describes her sex life in great detail, from masturbation to her experiences of group sex and sexual submission. This book, published in 2001 in France, was considered one of the most explicit books about sex ever written by a woman. Millet is one of the most famous people to have signed the anti-#MeToo op-ed in *Le Monde*.

2. In *The Possession* (trans. Anna Moschovakis [New York: Seven Stories Press, 2008]), French novelist Annie Ernaux describes how, over the course of six months, the narrator is occupied and invaded by the obsessive thoughts she has about her former partner after finding out he is moving in with someone else.

3. I decided to keep the transitive use of the verb "to think" here, although it is uncommon in English. The French transitive use communicates that thinking is an activity, sometimes interrogating a concept, sometimes reflecting on lived experience, sometimes understanding a phenomenon. "Penser" is not only about concepts and comprehension but also about reflection, observation, and experience.

4. Jean-Jacques Rousseau, *On The Social Contract*, in *The Major Political Writings of Jean-Jacques Rousseau*, ed. John T. Scott (Chicago: University of Chicago Press, 2012), 168.

5. "The Sexual Aberrations" (1905), "A Child Is Being Beaten" (1919), and "The Economic Problem of Masochism" (1924).

6. See, for instance, the way Rousseau conceives of the education of Sophie in Book V of *Émile, or, On Education*, trans. Allan Bloom (New York: Basic Books, 1979).

7. There are few exceptions, such as Andrea Dworkin (*Right-Wing Women* [New York: Peringee Books, 1983]) and Saba Mahmood (*Politics of Piety: The Islamic Revival and the Feminist Subject*, 2nd ed. [Princeton: Princeton University Press, 2012]).

8. The analyses that follow come from the work of Sally Haslanger in "Ideology, Generics, and Common Ground," in *Feminist Metaphysics: Explorations in the Ontology of Sex, Gender and the Self*, ed. Charlotte Witt (Dordrecht: Springer Netherlands, 2011), 179–207.

9. See, for instance, Sandra Harding, "Rethinking Standpoint Epistemology: What Is 'Strong Objectivity'?" in *Feminist Epistemologies*, ed. Linda Alcoff and Elizabeth Potter (New York: Routledge, 1993).

10. Susan M. Okin, *Women and Western Political Thought* (Princeton: Princeton University Press, 1978); Carole Pateman, *The Sexual Contract* (Stanford: Stanford University Press, 1988).

11. There is a debate about the Islamic veil, especially in France, regarding whether women are being submissive by wearing it—if they are submitting themselves to a patriarchal order by the very fact of wearing it. The 2004 law that bans headscarves in French schools rests on the idea that wearing a veil is a manifestation of patriarchal oppression. French activist Fadela Amara thus said "the veil is the visible symbol of the subjugation of women" and thus the law is justified: because girls attending school are minors, the state has the responsibility to protect them from subjection ("Ghetto Warrior," *Guardian*, July 17, 2006).

12. On the tension between French republicanism and the Islamic veil, see Cécile Laborde, *Critical Republicanism: The Hijab Controversy and Political Philosophy* (Oxford: Oxford University Press, 2008).

13. The distinction between the other and the Other is important in understanding the traditional conception of femininity. I will return to it in detail in the next chapters.

14. Abbie Goldberg, Julianna Smith, and Maureen Perry-Jenkins, "The Division of Labor in Lesbian, Gay, and Heterosexual New Adoptive Parents," *Journal of Marriage and Family* 74, no. 4 (2012): 812–28.

15. I do not mean to imply that the West is homogeneous, but I do think that the countries of North America and Europe have historical, cultural, and economic similarities, which can justify grouping them. In particular, my main concern here is the way imperialism and capitalism can create harmful "othering," and in that regard these countries are on the same side of both axes.

16. Uma Narayan, *Dislocating Cultures: Identities, Traditions, and Third-World Feminism* (New York: Routledge, 1997).

17. Uma Narayan, "Minds of Their Own: Choices, Autonomy, Cultural Practices, and Other Women," in *A Mind of One's Own: Feminist Essays on Reason and Objectivity*, ed. Louise M. Antony and Charlotte Witt (Boulder, CO: Westview, 1993; New York: Routledge, 2002), 418–32.

18. I particularly recommend Serene Khader, *Decolonizing Feminism: A Transnational Feminist Ethic* (New York: Oxford University Press, 2019).

19. "To dominate oneself" is used to signify self-mastery, but this use does not introduce the same kind of ambiguity for the verb "to dominate" as the transitive and pronominal uses of "to submit" insofar as the adopted perspective on power relations does not change.

20. In French, this conflation is even stronger as the same word (*soumis*) is used for "submissive" and "submitted".

21. This does not mean that I think the problem of female submission cannot be addressed through contemporary feminist philosophy, just that I believe a close reading of Beauvoir is a good way of analyzing this problem.

22. Gallimard, the French publisher of *The Second Sex*, is famous for the secrecy it maintains regarding the sales of its books. However, in just a few weeks after its publication, 22,000 copies of *The Second Sex* were sold; more than a million copies of the book were sold in France alone; and it has been translated into over forty languages.

23. Some notable exceptions are Sonia Kruks, *Simone de Beauvoir and the Politics of Ambiguity* (New York: Oxford University Press, 2012); Nancy Bauer, *How to Do Things with Pornography* (Cambridge, MA: Harvard University Press, 2015); and Lori Marso, *Politics with Beauvoir: Freedom in the Encounter* (Durham: Duke University Press, 2017).

24. The idea that Beauvoir is a philosopher, and not just a novelist, a quaint relic of feminism, and Sartre's girlfriend, is far from widely accepted. This book, in its French version, thus also aimed to convince French readers that Beauvoir is a philosopher and that the reluctance to see her as such is a manifestation of the sexism of the philosophical institution.

Chapter 2. Is Submission Feminine? Is Femininity a Submission?

1. In the context of American slavery, the question of responsibility with regard to submission is not as simple as in the example of the warrior. As Malcolm X's "Message to the Grassroots" shows, the derogatory connotation of the "house negro" epithet, and more generally the opposition between "house negro" and "field negro," reveals the complexities regarding the responsibility one bears in submission.

2. See, for instance, Paula Caplan, *The Myth of Women's Masochism* (New York: Dutton, 1985).

3. This development on the psychopathology of masochism owes a great deal to the analyses of Julie Mazaleigue-Labaste in "Preface: Le 'maudit problème du masochisme,'" in Sigmund Freud, *Du masochisme* (Paris: Payot, 2011), 7–45.

4. "At the same time as this process of repression takes place, a sense of guilt appears. This is also of unknown origin, but there is no doubt whatever that it is connected with the incestuous wishes, and that it is justified by the persistence of those wishes in the unconscious." Sigmund Freud, "'A Child Is Being Beaten': A Contribution to the Study of the Origin of Sexual Perversions" (1919), in *The Standard Edition of the Complete Psychological Works of Sigmund Freud*, vol. XVII (1917–1919): *An Infantile Neurosis and Other Works* (London: Hogarth Press, 1955), 186.

5. Ibid., 196.

6. Ibid., 197.

7. Sigmund Freud, "The Economic Problem of Masochism" (1924), in *The Standard Edition of the Complete Psychological Works of Sigmund Freud*, vol. XIX (1923–1925): *The Ego and the Id and Other Works* (London: Hogarth Press, 1961), 160.

8. He briefly justifies this omission—which consists in renouncing to explain masochism since it does not account for what is precisely mysterious about it—by a principle of economy: he thus writes about pain in pleasure that it "cannot be explained without taking our discussion very far back" (ibid., 161).

9. Ibid., 164.

10. Eph. 5:21–34, King James Version.

11. Surah 4, verse 34. English translation by Seyyed Hossein Nasr, ed., *The Study Quran* (New York: Harper and Collins, 2015).

12. On the issues raised by a patriarchal reading of the Quran, see Asma Barlas, *Believing Women in Islam: Unreading Patriarchal Interpretations of the Quran* (Austin: University of Texas Press, 2002).

13. Rousseau, *Émile, or, On Education*, 364–65, 369.

14. Catharine MacKinnon, *Toward a Feminist Theory of the State* (Cambridge, MA: Harvard University Press, 1989), 219.

15. Catharine MacKinnon, "Sexuality, Pornography, and Method: Pleasure under Patriarchy," *Ethics* 99, no. 2 (January 1989): 316.

16. "The normal sexual aim is regarded as being the union of the genitals in the act known as copulation, which leads to a release of the sexual tension and a temporary extinction of the sexual instinct—a satisfaction analogous to the sating of hunger." Sigmund Freud, "The Sexual Aberrations," in *Three Essays on the Theory of Sexuality* in *The Standard Edition of the Complete Psychological Works of Sigmund Freud*, vol. VII (1901–1905): *A Case of Hysteria, Three Essays on Sexuality and Other Works* (London: Hogarth Press and the Institute of Psychoanalysis, 1953), 148.

17. MacKinnon, "Sexuality, Pornography, and Method," 315.

18. Ibid., 333–34.

19. Ibid., 318–19.

20. MacKinnon, *Toward a Feminist Theory of the State*, 113–14.

21. "In radical feminism, the condition of the sexes and the relevant definition of women as a group is conceived as social down to the somatic level. Only incidentally, perhaps even consequentially, is it biological" (ibid., 46).

22. "On the first day that matters, dominance was achieved, probably by force." Catharine MacKinnon, *Feminism Unmodified: Discourses on Life and Law* (Cambridge, MA: Harvard University Press, 1987), 40.

23. According to MacKinnon, her theory, which she names "the dominance approach," seeks to mitigate the insufficiencies of an egalitarian theory of difference. In her view, the relegation of women to very poorly paid employment and the immense prevalence of rape, domestic violence, prostitution, and pornography constitute a type of abuse to which women qua women are confronted and that the egalitarian approach of sexual difference does not address in a legal manner. Indeed, insofar as they concern almost exclusively women, these types of abuse are not problematic in terms of equality with men. The approach in terms of domination allows, to the contrary, justifying a systematic approach to these issues on a legal dimension, as it appears clearly in the law casebook of almost two thousand pages published by MacKinnon on these issues: *Sex Equality*, 3rd ed., University Casebook Series (St. Paul: Foundation Press, 2016).

24. To my knowledge, MacKinnon does not justify this choice anywhere.

25. In that sense, their submission is does not come from submitting themselves. They are submitted in the same way war prisoners are according to Hobbes, when they have no other choice than submission or death.

Chapter 3. Womanhood as a Situation

1. "In fact, I wanted to write about myself. I liked Leiris' *L'Âge d'homme*; such sacrificial essays, in which the author strips himself bare without excuses appealed to me. I let the idea begin to take shape, made a few notes, and talked to Sartre about it. I realized that the first question to come up was: What has it meant to me to be a woman? . . . 'For me', I said to Sartre, 'you might almost say it just hasn't counted.' 'All the same, you weren't brought up in the same way as a boy would have been; you should look into it further.'

I looked, and it was a revelation: this world was a masculine world, my childhood had been nourished by myths forged by men, and I hadn't reacted to them in at all the same way as I would have done if I had been a boy. I was so interested in this that I abandoned my project for a personal confession in order to give all my attention to finding out about the feminine condition in its generality. I went to the Bibliothèque

Nationale to do some readings and I studied the myths of femininity." Simone de Beauvoir, *Force of Circumstance*, trans. Richard Howard (London: Readers Union Andre Deutsch and Wiedenfeld and Nicolson, 1966), 94–95, translation modified.

This anecdote should not be seen as proof that Beauvoir had never had the idea of writing about femininity and womanhood before this conversation, as Kate Kirkpatrick remarkably demonstrates in her biography *Becoming Beauvoir: A Life* (London: Bloomsbury, 2019).

2. For a more detailed analysis of this topic, see, for instance, Alison Stone, "Essentialism and Anti-Essentialism in Feminist Philosophy," *Journal of Moral Philosophy*, no 1.2 (2004): 135–53.

3. Simone de Beauvoir, *The Second Sex*, trans. Constance Borde and Sheila Malovany-Chevallier (New York: Vintage Books, 2011), 3.

4. Ibid., 4.

5. Ibid.

6. "Queer" historically has been the slur used to describe gender-nonconforming people, and it has been reappropriated by them into a positive description of their identity.

7. Because Beauvoir writes before the creation of the sex/gender distinction and because the introduction of this distinction obscures the substance of Beauvoir's thesis, I will avoid as much as possible using the term "gender" in this book when I refer to Beauvoir's work, without it meaning that sex difference would be biologically grounded.

8. Beauvoir, *The Second Sex*, 4.

9. Judith Butler, "Sex and Gender in Simone de Beauvoir's *Second Sex*," *Yale French Studies* 72 (1986): 35–49.

10. Beauvoir, *The Second Sex*, 283.

11. "The balance of productive and reproductive forces is different depending on the different economic moments of human history, and they condition the relation of the male and the female to children and consequently among them. But we are then going beyond the field of biology: with biology only, it would not be possible to posit the primacy of one sex concerning the role it plays in perpetuating the species.

At any rate, a society is not a species: in society the species realizes itself as existence: it transcends itself towards the world and towards the future, its customs cannot be deduced from biology; the individuals are never left to their nature; they obey this second nature that custom is and in which the desires and fears that express their ontological attitude are reflected. It is not as a body but as a body subjected to taboos, to laws, that the subject gains consciousness of and accomplishes itself; it is in the name of certain values that he valorizes himself. And once again, physiology cannot ground values: rather, biological data takes on the values the existent confers to them" (ibid., 47).

12. "Some essential biological givens are not part of her lived situation: for example, the structure of the ovum is not reflected in it; by contrast, an organ of slight

biological importance like the clitoris plays a primary role in it. Nature does not define the woman: it is she who defines herself by reclaiming nature for herself in her affectivity" (ibid., 49).

13. For a precise analysis of social constructionism, see Sally Haslanger, "Ontology and Social Construction," *Philosophical Topics* 23, no. 2 (Fall 1995): 95–125.

14. Beauvoir, *The Second Sex*, 12–13.

15. "The given in no way enters into the constitution of freedom since freedom is interiorized as the internal negation of the given. It is simply the pure contingency which freedom exerts by denying the given while making itself a choice; the given is the plenitude of being which freedom colors with insufficiency and with négatité by illuminating it with the light of an end which does not exist. The given is freedom itself in so far as freedom exists; and whatever it does, freedom cannot escape its existence. . . . Thus by its very projection toward an end, freedom constitutes as a being in the midst of the world a particular datum which it has to be. Freedom does not choose it, for this would be to choose its own existence; but by the choice which it makes of its end, freedom causes the datum to be revealed in this or that way, in this or that light in connection with the revelation of the world itself. . . . We shall use the term situation for the contingency of freedom in the *plenum* of being of the world inasmuch as this *datum*, which is there only in order not to constrain freedom, is revealed to this freedom only as already illuminated by the end which freedom chooses." Jean-Paul Sartre, *Being and Nothingness*, trans. Hazel Barnes (New York: Philosophical Library, 1956), 613.

16. "What unity do we find in these various aspects of bad faith? It is a certain art of forming contradictory concepts which unite in themselves both an idea and the negation of that idea. The basic concept which is thus engendered, utilizes the double property of the human being, who is at once a facticity and a transcendence. These two aspects of human reality are and ought to be capable of a valid coordination. But bad faith does not wish either to coordinate them nor to surmount them in a synthesis. Bad faith seeks to affirm their identity while preserving their differences. It must affirm facticity as being transcendence and transcendence as being facticity, in such a way that at the instant when a person apprehends the one, he can find himself abruptly faced with the other" (ibid., 131).

17. Simone de Beauvoir, *The Prime of Life*, trans. Peter Green (New York: Penguin, 1965), 434, translation modified. It is interesting to note how even in Beauvoir's work, the reflection on female submission is inseparable from the orientalist cliché of the harem.

18. "My life ceased to be a game, I knew what my roots were, and I no longer pretended I could escape my own human condition. Instead, I endeavored to bear it. Henceforth I took reality at its proper weight and valuation. At times I found it repugnant to accept it" (ibid., 600).

19. In the "Présentation" of the first issue of *Les Temps modernes*, the journal of opinion Sartre and Beauvoir founded with Merleau-Ponty, Raymond Aron, and others,

Sartre elaborated the idea of "commitment" and "committed literature" (*littérature engagée*): he claimed that failing to include a political dimension in literature and the arts was supporting the current state of the world.

20. Simone de Beauvoir, *The Ethics of Ambiguity*, trans. Bernard Frechtman (New York: Citadel Press, 1976), 38, translation modified.

21. Beauvoir, *The Prime of Life*, 478.

22. I here use the pronoun "they" as an epicene (gender-neutral) singular pronoun to refer to the Dasein in order to avoid gendering them since Dasein is in a way the human being before any facticity like sex is attributed to it. Martin Heidegger, *Being and Time*, 1927, trans. John Macquarrie and Edward Robinson (London: SCM Press, 1962), §4, p. 32 [12].

23. Ibid., 119 [86].

24. "The 'they' has its own ways in which to be" (Sartre, *Being and Nothingness*, 164 [127]). (Instead of following the translation of Macquarrie and Robinson, I agree with Hubert Dreyfus that the German "das Man" is better translated as "the 'one'" than "the 'they.'")

25. Beauvoir, *The Second Sex*, 4.

26. Ibid.

27. Beauvoir started reading Marx in 1931: "I wanted to understand Marx and Engels, and started in on *Das Kapital* at the Bibliothèque Nationale. This was not a success on my part. I made no distinction between Marxism and any other philosophy to which I had become accustomed: so much so, indeed, that the whole thing seemed immediately comprehensible to me, and in fact I grasped almost none of it. Nevertheless, the theory of surplus value came as a revelation to me, a revelation as dazzling as the Cartesian *Cogito* or Kant's critique of space and time. . . . A new day dawned upon my world at the instant that I saw labor as the source and substance of all values. Nothing was ever to make me deny this truth: not the objections which the final sections of *Das Kapital* aroused in me, nor those which I found in other books, nor even the subtle doctrines propounded by more recent economists" (*The Prime of Life*, 51, translation modified).

She continued reading Marxist literature through the 1930s. She thus writes, around 1933: "Economic and social problems interested me, but only from the theoretical angle . . . I read Marx, and Rosa Luxemburg, and Trotsky's *The History of the Russian Revolution*, and *Piatiletka*, Farbman's work on the Five-Year Plan, besides various studies on the economy of the NEP, the life of the American workingman, and the crisis in England" (ibid., 147).

28. "However, in Marxism, if it is true that the goal and the meaning of action are defined by human wills, these wills do not appear as free. They are the reflection of objective conditions by which the situation of the class or the people under consideration is defined. . . . Subjectivity is re-absorbed into the objectivity of the given world. Revolt, need, hope, rejection, and desire are only the resultants of external forces. The psychology of behavior endeavors to explain this alchemy.

It is known that that is the essential point on which existentialist ontology is opposed to dialectical materialism. We think that the meaning of the situation is not to impose itself on the consciousness of a passive subject, that it surges up only by the disclosure which a free subject effects in his project" (Beauvoir, *The Ethics of Ambiguity*, 19–20).

29. Ibid., 47–48.

30. For instance, Beauvoir writes in the conclusion of *The Second Sex*: "The wrong does not come from individual perversity—and bad faith arises when each people attack the other—it comes from a situation in the face of which all individual behavior is powerless" (760).

31. Ibid., 4.

32. Ibid.

33. Ibid., 279.

Chapter 4. Elusive Submission

1. See Kristie Dotson, "How Is This Paper Philosophy?" *Comparative Philosophy* 3, no. 1 (2012): 3–29.

2. Friedrich Nietzsche, *The Gay Science*, trans. Walter Kaufmann (New York: Vintage Books, 1974), §355, pp. 301–2.

3. For an in-depth analysis of the problem this raises for philosophy, one can look at the works of the philosopher Sandra Laugier.

4. See Beauvoir, *Force of Circumstance*.

5. See note 3 in chapter 1.

6. James C. Scott, *Domination and the Arts of Resistance: Hidden Transcripts* (New Haven: Yale University Press, 1990), 18.

7. The expression "histoire événementielle" was borrowed by Fernand Braudel from François Simiand. Braudel uses this expression to distinguish three time spans that historians should take into account. "Histoire événementielle" can be translated as "history of events," "episodic history," or "evental history," and it refers to the historiographical practice consisting in focusing mainly on the succession of events, often of political events, instead of studying long-term structures or social history.

8. Even if it is not directly attached to the Annales school, E. P. Thompson's *The Making of the English Working Class* (New York: Vintage, 1966) demonstrates the same commitment to inverting the usual perspective on power.

9. Michel Foucault, *"Society Must Be Defended": Lectures at the Collège de France, 1975–76*, trans. David Macey (New York: Picador, 2003).

10. "When I say 'subjugated knowledges' I am also referring to a whole series of knowledges that have been disqualified as nonconceptual knowledges, as insufficiently elaborated knowledges. . . . And it is thanks to the reappearance of these knowledges from below, of these unqualified or even disqualified knowledges, it is thanks to the

reappearance of these knowledges: the knowledge of the psychiatrized, the patient, the nurse, the doctor, that is parallel to, marginal to, medical knowledge, . . . it is the reappearance of what people know at a local level, of these disqualified knowledges, that made the critique possible" (ibid., 7–8).

11. Jane Austen, *Northanger Abbey*, vol. 1, chapter 14, in Barbara M. Benedict and Deirdre Le Faye, *The Cambridge Edition of the Works of Jane Austen* (Cambridge: Cambridge University Press, 2006), 109–10.

12. See, for instance, Michelle Perrot and Georges Duby, eds., *History of Women in the West*, 5 vols. (Cambridge, MA: Harvard University Press, 1992–94).

13. It is, of course, possible to find oneself in such a hierarchically inferior position without submitting oneself. Several works in anthropology and sociology on this issue show that resistance to domination is largely underestimated because domination is generally studied by dominants who see their successes more clearly than their failures. See works by James C. Scott, particularly *Domination and the Arts of Resistance*.

14. Gayatri Spivak, "Can the Subaltern Speak?" in *Marxism and the Interpretation of Culture*, ed. Cary Nelson and Lawrence Grossberg (New York: MacMillan, 1988), 271–313.

15. "Intellectuals and Power," first published in Donald F. Bouchard, ed., *Language, Counter-Memory, Practice: Selected Essays and Interviews by Michel Foucault* (Ithaca: Cornell University Press, 1977), 205–17.

16. Ibid., 209, translation modified.

17. Spivak, "Can the Subaltern Speak?" 272.

18. Part of Spivak's reflection, in this text as in others, concerns the difference between the oppressed and the subaltern. In an interview in 1992 she explained: "Subaltern is [not] just a classy word for 'oppressed', for Other, for somebody who's not getting a piece of the pie. . . . everything that has limited or no access to the cultural imperialism is subaltern—a space of difference. Now, who would say that's just the oppressed? The working class is oppressed. It's not subaltern." Leon de Kock, "Interview with Gayatri Chakravorty Spivak: New Nation Writers Conference in South Africa," *ARIEL: A Review of International English Literature* 3, no. 23 (1992): 29–47, quote on 45–46.

19. Spivak, "Can the Subaltern Speak?" 295.

Chapter 5. The Experience of Submission

1. There are good reasons to believe that Beauvoir is, consciously or not, here inspired by W.E.B. Du Bois and the way he analyzed his position as both an outsider and an insider. During her trip to the United States in 1947, she became close to Richard Wright, who introduced her to Du Bois and many other Black writers. See Margaret Simons, "Richard Wright, Simone de Beauvoir and *The Second Sex*," in *Beauvoir and* The Second Sex: *Feminism, Race, and the Origins of Existentialism* (Lanham,

MD: Rowman and Littlefield, 1999). Her understanding of women's oppression is deeply influenced by her readings on the problem of race in the United States and, in return, deeply influenced other theorists of race, especially Fanon. On this, see Mathieu Renault, "Le genre de la race: Fanon, lecteur de Beauvoir," *Actuel Marx* 1, no. 55 (2014): 36–48.

2. Beauvoir, *The Second Sex*, 15.

3. Beauvoir, *Force of Circumstance*, 189.

4. Beauvoir, *The Second Sex*, 748, translation modified.

5. See, for instance, Sonia Kruks, *Situation and Human Existence: Freedom, Subjectivity, and Society* (London: Unwin Hyman, 1990), 111; Karen Vintges, *Philosophy as Passion: The Thinking of Simone de Beauvoir* (Bloomington: Indiana University Press, 1996), 136–59; Sara Heinämaa, *Toward a Phenomenology of Sexual Difference: Husserl, Merleau-Ponty, Beauvoir* (Lanham, MD: Rowman and Littlefield, 2003), xiii.

6. Beauvoir, *The Prime of Life*, 135, translation modified.

7. Edmund Husserl, *Die Krisis der europäischen Wissenschaften und die transzendentale Phänomenologie, Husserliana, Band VI.*, ed. Walter Biemel (Haag: Martinus Nijhoff, 1950–52), 62. On the appropriation of Husserl's method by Beauvoir, see Sara Heinämaa's work, particularly "Simone de Beauvoir's Phenomenology of Sexual Difference," *Hypatia* 14, no. 4 (Autumn 1999): 114–32.

8. As we will see in chapter 7, Beauvoir's philosophy of the body is deeply influenced by Merleau-Ponty.

9. Beauvoir, *The Second Sex*, 17.

10. Ibid., 279, translation modified.

11. "Only then can we understand what problems women—heirs to a weighty past, striving to forge a new future—are faced with" (ibid.).

12. Quoted by Beauvoir in *Force of Circumstance*, 187. François Mauriac was probably the most important conservative intellectual at the time. This is one of the many examples of the sexism Beauvoir encountered when *The Second Sex* was released.

13. "When it came to the second volume, I also profited from the continual interest in people that Sartre and I had had for so many years; my memory provided me with an abundance of material" (ibid., 186, translation modified).

14. That is to say she refuses to adopt the perspective of what Husserl calls the "transcendental ego."

15. See, for instance, Beauvoir, *The Second Sex*, 440–41.

16. She thus sketches, in the first volume, the necessity of a third way, between individualism and a structural approach, when she writes: "Underlying the individual tragedies as well as the economic history of humanity, there is an existential infrastructure that alone makes it possible to understand in its unity this singular form that is a life" (ibid., 68, translation modified).

17. On the issue of the inversion of perspective and the methodological issues it raises, see chapters 1 and 4.

18. It goes without saying that the framing of the issue in terms of top-down versus bottom-up epistemology is foreign (and posterior) to Beauvoir.

19. Bruno Frère and Sébastien Laoureux, eds., *La Phénoménologie à l'usage des sciences humaines* (Brussels: Peter Lang, 2013), 9.

20. Beauvoir, *The Second Sex*, 17, translation modified.

21. Ibid., 483–84.

22. Ibid., 474–75.

23. The concept of intersectionality was first conceived of as a metaphor used in a legal context to mitigate the problems of antidiscrimination law. Legal theorist Kimberlé Crenshaw created this concept to address the fact that antidiscrimination law was written such that Black women who were filing a lawsuit had to determine whether they were being discriminated against qua women or qua Black, which made the specific discrimination they were suffering from as Black women invisible. This concept has been used more broadly to think the relations between different systems of oppression.

24. Judith Okely, *Simone de Beauvoir: A Re-Reading* (London: Virago, 1986).

25. On the racist and classist dimensions of this hypothesis among white feminists from the 1950s to the 1970s, see bell hooks's works, especially *Feminist Theory from Margin to Center* (Boston: South End Press, 1984). The best-known critique of Beauvoir as a second wave feminist is found in Elizabeth Spelman, *Inessential Women: Problems of Exclusion in Feminist Thought* (Boston: Beacon Press, 1988).

26. On the reception of *The Second Sex*, see Toril Moi, *Simone de Beauvoir: The Making of an Intellectual Woman*, 2nd ed. (Oxford: Oxford University Press, 2008) and Ingrid Galster, ed., *Le Deuxième Sexe de Simone de Beauvoir* (Paris: Presses de l'université Paris-Sorbonne, 2004).

27. This is the main thesis defended (brilliantly) by Nancy Bauer in *Simone de Beauvoir, Philosophy, and Feminism* (New York: Columbia University Press, 2001).

Chapter 6. Submission Is an Alienation

1. "There are deep analogies between the situations of women and blacks: both liberate themselves today from the same paternalism, and the former master caste wants to keep them 'in their place,' that is, the place chosen for them; in both cases, they praise, more or less sincerely, the virtues of the 'good black,' the carefree, childlike, merry soul of the resigned black, and the woman who is a 'true woman'—frivolous, infantile, irresponsible, the woman who submits to man" (Beauvoir, *The Second Sex*, 12).

2. See Kathryn Gines, "Comparative and Competing Frameworks of Oppression in Simone de Beauvoir's *The Second Sex*," *Graduate Faculty Philosophy Journal* 35, no. 1 (2014): 251–73.

3. "6 July . . . I went to the Bibliothèque Nationale. I took a reader's pass and I have started reading Hegel, the *Phenomenology of Spirit*. At present, I can scarcely make

head or tail of a word of it. I have decided to work at Hegel every afternoon from two till five. It's the most soothing occupation I can imagine" (Beauvoir, *The Prime of Life*, 456, translation modified).

4. Beauvoir, *The Second Sex*, 7.

5. This claim has one exception: according to Beauvoir, the tyranny that the married wife sometimes exerts on her husband is comparable to the master-slave dialectic since the husband is oppressed because of the oppression he exerts: "The master-slave dialectic has its most concrete application here: in oppressing, one becomes oppressed. Males are in chains by their very sovereignty; it is because they alone earn money that the wife demands checks, because men alone practice a profession that the wife demands that they succeed, because they alone embody transcendence that the wife wants to steal it from them by taking over their projects and successes. And inversely, the tyranny wielded by the woman only manifests her dependence: . . . if she bitterly seeks to subjugate him to her will, it is because she is alienated in him" (ibid., 522, translation modified).

6. "Mastery arises from the Struggle to death for 'recognition' (*Anerkennung*). The two opponents each posit for themselves an end that is essentially human, non-animal and non-biological: that of being 'recognised' in their human reality or dignity. But the future Master endures the trial of Struggle and Risk, while the future Slave fails to control his (animal) fear of death. He thus surrenders, recognises his defeat, recognises the superiority of the victor and subjugates himself as a Slave to his Master. This is how the absolute Authority of the Master arises in his relations with his Slave." Alexandre Kojève, *The Notion of Authority (A Brief Presentation)*, trans. Hager Weslati (London: Verso, 2014), 42.

7. Beauvoir, *The Second Sex*, 8.

8. Beauvoir locates the foundation of this subordination in the burden that constitutes motherhood and the impossibility of controlling fertility until the twentieth century.

9. "Therefore, it is by work, and only by work, that man *realizes* himself *objectively* as a man." Alexandre Kojève, *Introduction to the Reading of Hegel: Lectures on the* Phenomenology of Spirit, trans. James H. Nichols (Ithaca: Cornell University Press, 1969), 25.

10. Beauvoir, *The Second Sex*, 474–75.

11. On this topic, see Eva Lundgren-Gothlin, *Sex and Existence: Simone de Beauvoir's* The Second Sex (Hanover, NH: University Press of New England, 1996).

12. Beauvoir, *The Second Sex*, 6, translation modified.

13. "But women are not a minority like American blacks, or like Jews: there are as many women as men on the earth. Often, the two opposing groups concerned were once independent of each other; either they were not aware of each other in the past, or they accepted each other's autonomy; and some historical event subordinated the weaker to the stronger: the Jewish Diaspora, slavery in America, and the colonial

conquests are facts with dates. In these cases, for the oppressed there was a before" (ibid., 7–8).

14. Kathryn Gines is right to show that the comparison with Blacks, Jews, and proletarians rests on an implicit negation of the possibility of multiple identities. However we can see here that her claim that Beauvoir does not think the possibility of women that would not be white and bourgeois does not adequately reflect Beauvoir's work. Gines, "Comparative and Competing Frameworks of Oppression in Simone de Beauvoir's *The Second Sex*."

15. Beauvoir, *The Second Sex*, 8–9, translation modified.

16. Nancy Bauer, "Being-with as Being-against: Heidegger Meets Hegel in *The Second Sex*," *Continental Philosophy Review* 34 (2001): 132.

17. Beauvoir, *The Second Sex*, 7.

18. Ibid., 159–60.

19. Ibid., 270.

20. Ibid.

21. Ibid., 162.

22. Catharine MacKinnon, "Feminism, Marxism, Method and the State: An Agenda for Theory," *Signs* 7, no. 3 (1982): 537–38.

23. Beauvoir, *The Second Sex*, 17, translation modified.

Chapter 7. The Objectified Body of the Submissive Woman

1. This part of the analysis is indebted to the remarkable work done by Nancy Bauer in *Simone de Beauvoir, Philosophy, and Feminism*, chap. 2.

2. "If I want to define myself, I first have to say, 'I am a woman'; this truth is the background on which any other assertion will arise" (Beauvoir, *The Second Sex*, 5, translation modified).

3. Iris Marion Young, *Throwing Like a Girl and Other Essays in Feminist Philosophy and Social Theory* (Bloomington: Indiana University Press, 1990).

4. Beauvoir, *The Second Sex*, 44.

5. Ibid., 48.

6. "The male's sex life is normally integrated into his individual existence: in terms of desire and coitus, his surpassing toward the species is an integral part of the subjective moment of his transcendence: he is his body. Woman's history is much more complex" (ibid., 39).

7. Ibid., 40.

8. Ibid., 42.

9. Ibid., 44.

10. Ibid., 42.

11. Ibid.

12. Ibid., 41. Beauvoir here adds a note in which she quotes Merleau-Ponty: "I am thus my body, at least inasmuch as I have experience, and reciprocally, my body is like a natural subject, like a tentative draft of my total being" (Maurice Merleau-Ponty, *Phenomenology of Perception*, trans. Colin Smith [London: Routledge Classics, 2002]).

13. See, for instance, Charlene H. Seigfried, "Second Sex: Second Thoughts," in *Hypatia Reborn: Essays in Feminist Philosophy*, ed. Azizah Y. al-Hibri and Margaret Simons (Bloomington: Indiana University Press, 1990), 305–22; Catriona Mackenzie, "Simone de Beauvoir: Philosophy and/or the Female Body," in *Feminist Challenges: Social and Political Theory*, ed. Carole Pateman and Elizabeth Gross (Sydney: Allen and Unwin, 1986), 144–56.

14. Beauvoir, *The Second Sex*, 47–48.

15. Ibid., 48.

16. Ibid., 762.

17. "It is the making explicit or bringing to light of the prescientific life of consciousness which alone endows scientific operations with meaning and to which these latter always refer back" (Merleau-Ponty, *Phenomenology of Perception*, 68).

18. Beauvoir, *The Second Sex*, 46, translation modified.

19. Ibid., 49.

20. Ibid., 44.

21. Ibid., 43, translation modified.

22. On the analysis of alienation in *The Second Sex* and its role in Beauvoir's philosophy of the body, see Toril Moi, "Ambiguous Women: Alienation and the Body in *The Second Sex*," in *Simone de Beauvoir: The Making of an Intellectual Woman*, 168–97.

23. Beauvoir, *The Second Sex*, 538.

24. Ibid., 42.

25. Ibid., 41.

26. Ibid., 35, 41, 43, 304, 335, 349.

27. Ibid., 42, 44, 285, 296.

28. Ibid., 73, 305, 342, 347.

29. Sartre, *Being and Nothingness*, 221.

30. Ibid., 236.

31. Ibid., 256.

32. Ibid., 305.

33. Ibid., 302.

34. I am indebted to two analyses of Sartre's philosophy: Renaud Barbaras, "Le corps et la chair dans la troisième partie de *L'Être et le Néant*," in *Sartre et la phénoménologie*, ed. Jean-Marc Mouillie (Paris: ENS Éditions, 2000), 279–96; Kim Sang Ong-Van-Cung, "Le corps et l'expérience d'autrui: Un aspect du problème de la négation dans *L'Être et le Néant*," in *Sartre. L'Être et le Néant. Nouvelles lectures*, ed. Jean-Marc Mouillie and Jean-Philippe Narboux (Paris: Les Belles Lettres, 2015), 115–36.

35. "Either it is a thing among other things, or else it is that by which things are revealed to me. But it can not be both at the same time" (Sartre, *Being and Nothingness*, 304).

36. "This object exists for us only in the capacity of an indication; it is what everything indicates to me and what on principle I cannot apprehend since it is what I *am*" (ibid., 317–18).

37. Ibid., 535.

38. Ibid., 364.

39. In the first pages of the part on myths, Beauvoir reaffirms the validity of the idea of a conflict of consciousnesses, but she uses strictly Hegelian terms. According to her, men are trying to escape the danger of this conflict through the constitution of the woman as Other: "She pits neither the hostile silence of nature nor the hard demand of a reciprocal recognition against him; by a unique privilege she is a consciousness, and yet it seems possible to possess her in the flesh. Thanks to her, there is a way to escape the inexorable dialectic of the master and the slave that springs from the reciprocity of freedoms" (Beauvoir, *The Second Sex*, 160).

40. For an account of a morally neutral sexual objectification, see Martha Nussbaum, "Objectification," *Philosophy & Public Affairs* 24, no. 4 (October 1995): 249–91.

41. Beauvoir, *The Second Sex*, 161.

42. Ibid., 160.

43. Ibid., 320.

44. Ibid., 321, translation modified.

45. Ibid.

46. I am thinking here particularly of Fiona Vera-Gray, who uses Beauvoirian analyses to interpret the empiric research she did on the first experiences girls have of street harassment. Fiona Vera-Gray, *Men's Intrusion, Women's Embodiment: A Critical Analysis of Street Harassment* (London: Routledge, 2016).

47. Beauvoir, *The Second Sex*, 370, translation modified.

48. Jean-Jacques Rousseau, *Confessions*, book 1, in Jean-Jacques Rousseau, *The Confessions and Correspondence, Including the Letters to Malesherbes*, ed. Christopher Kelly, Roger Masters, and Peter Stillman (Hanover, NH: Dartmouth College Press, 1995).

Chapter 8. Delights or Oppression: The Ambiguity of Submission

1. Beauvoir, *The Second Sex*, 305.

2. Ibid., 572, translation modified.

3. Ibid.

4. Ibid., 575.

5. Ibid., 577, translation modified.

6. Beauvoir, *The Prime of Life*, 80, translation modified.

7. Simone de Beauvoir, *Memoirs of a Dutiful Daughter*, trans. James Kirkup (New York: Harper and Row, 1959), 344, translation modified.

8. Ibid., 339.

9. There are good reasons to think that, in her memoirs, Beauvoir pictures her relationship with Sartre as much more traditionally gendered than it actually was in order not to scare her middle-class female readership. On this hypothesis, see Kirkpatrick, *Becoming Beauvoir: A Life*.

10. "Yet I did not regard myself as a philosopher: I was well aware that the ease with which I penetrated to the heart of the text stemmed, precisely, from my lack of originality. . . . When I talked philosophy with Sartre, and took the full measure of his patience and audacity, the idea of a philosophical career seemed vividly exciting—but only if one was bitten by a theory of one's own. . . . When reading a work of Fink's I found myself wondering how anyone could bear to be someone else's follower, or disciple. Later I did, intermittently, come—for various reasons—to play such a role myself. But I had initially far too much intellectual ambition to let this satisfy me. I wanted to communicate what was original in my experience. In order to do so successfully, I knew it was literature towards which I must orientate myself" (Beauvoir, *The Prime of Life*, 221, translation modified).

11. About this, see the fascinating analyses of Margaret Simons in "Beauvoir, Philosophy, and Autobiography," in *A Companion to Simone de Beauvoir*, ed. Laura Hengehold and Nancy Bauer (Hoboken, NJ: John Wiley and Sons, 2017), 391–405.

12. Beauvoir, *The Second Sex*, 683.

13. "Men might be passionate lovers at certain moments of their existence, but there is not one who could be defined as 'a man in love'; in their most violent passions, they never fully abdicate; even if they fall on their knees before their mistress, they still wish to possess her, annex her; at the heart of their lives, they remain sovereign subjects; the woman they love is merely one value among others; they want to integrate her into their existence, not submerge their entire existence in her. By contrast, love for the woman is a total abdication for the benefit of a master" (ibid., translation modified).

14. Ibid., 684.

15. Ibid., 696.

16. Ibid., 305.

17. Ibid., 390.

18. Ibid., 684.

19. Ibid., 694, translation modified.

20. Ibid., 695.

21. Ibid., 699.

22. Simone de Beauvoir, *The Mandarins*, trans. Leonard Friedman (Cleveland: World Publishing Company, 1958), 53.

23. Ibid., 91.

24. Ibid.

25. Ibid., 404.

26. Beauvoir, *The Ethics of Ambiguity*, 25.

27. Beauvoir, *The Second Sex*, 390.

28. Ibid., 664.

29. Ibid., 470.

30. Ibid., 367.

31. Ibid., 305.

32. Ibid., 10.

33. On the inner colonization of women's minds by patriarchy, see Sandra Bartky, *Femininity and Domination: Studies in the Phenomenology of Oppression* (New York: Routledge, 1990).

Chapter 9. Freedom and Submission

1. Beauvoir, *The Second Sex*, 16, translation modified.

2. "At its imaginary level, Sartre's philosophy rests on his social experience as a man, a European, and a philosophy teacher which, taken as a whole, is an unequivocal experience of domination." Michèle Le Dœuff, *Hipparchia's Choice: An Essay Concerning Women, Philosophy, Etc.*, trans. Trista Selous (London: Blackwell, 1991), 75.

3. "This phenomenology establishes an ontological hierarchy: in this light woman can be assimilated to the In-itself and man to the For-itself, definitively and forever. The masculine and feminine roles deduced from these wooly theories make a non-subject of woman, who had already become an object when the object of knowledge (or rather 'the thing') was assimilated to 'the smooth whiteness of a woman's body'" (ibid., 82).

4. "No oppression is thinkable in the existentialist system and that of women no more than any other; secondly, this theory offers a space for expressing a terror on the part of men in relation to women's bodies which provides the basis of an ontological-carnal hierarchy between masculine and feminine" (ibid., 60).

5. Beauvoir, *The Second Sex*, 16.

6. Ibid.

7. "The problem is particularly acute in the context of entrenched inequalities and deprivations. A thoroughly deprived person, leading a very reduced life, might not appear to be badly off in terms of the mental metric of desire and its fulfilment, if the hardship is accepted with non-grumbling resignation. In situations of long-standing deprivation, the victims do not go on grieving and lamenting all the time, and very often make great efforts to take pleasure in small mercies and to cut down personal desires to modest—'realistic'—proportions. Indeed, in situations of adversity which

the victims cannot individually change, *prudential reasoning* would suggest that the victims should concentrate their desires on those limited things that they *can* possibly achieve, rather than fruitlessly pining for what is unattainable. The extent of a person's deprivation, then, may not at all show up in the metric of desire-fulfilment, even though he or she may be quite unable to be adequately nourished, decently clothed, minimally educated, and properly sheltered." Amartya Sen, *Inequality Reexamined* (New York: Russell Sage Foundation; Cambridge, MA: Harvard University Press, 1995), 55.

8. Sen had already developed this idea of a contradiction between welfare economics and social justice in "The Impossibility of a Paretian Liberal," *Journal of Political Economy* 78, no. 1 (1970): 152–57.

9. One of the main epistemic obstacles in adaptive preferences stems from the fact that the adaptive dimension of these preferences cannot be revealed. In other words, since choices are commonly held by economists to be the way in which preferences are revealed, it is impossible to know for sure how different the preferences of an individual would be without social domination. Therefore, there can be no proof that preferences have been adapted to a certain situation (at best, one can observe the correlation of a change of situation and a change of preferences). The way patriarchy, as a structure of social domination, works gives us good reason to expect that women adapt their preferences because of it.

10. Simone de Beauvoir, "Existentialism and Popular Wisdom," in *Simone de Beauvoir. Political Writings*, ed. Margaret Simons et al. (Urbana-Champaign: University of Illinois Press, 2014), 212.

11. Beauvoir, *The Ethics of Ambiguity*, 35ff.

12. "The child's situation is characterized by his finding himself cast into a universe which he has not helped to establish, which has been fashioned without him, and which appears to him as an absolute to which he can only submit" (ibid., 35).

13. Beauvoir here makes remarks on slavery that are not only politically problematic but also logically unsound since she denies slaves any form of agency, compares them to children, and, at the same time, represents them as "docilely submit[ing]" to planters (ibid., 37).

14. Ibid., 38, translation modified.

15. Ibid., 48–49, translation modified.

16. I use "cost-benefit analysis" in its everyday meaning of an analysis in which costs and benefits of a decision are weighed against each other, and not in the specific sense it has in well-being economics.

17. See, for instance, Alexandra Killewald and Margaret Gough, "Money Isn't Everything: Wives' Earnings and Housework Time," *Social Science Research* 39, no. 6 (2010): 987–1003.

18. An important distinction in contemporary political philosophy is the one between ideal and non-ideal theory. Ideal theory is a form of political philosophy that

focuses on thinking about just situations. A paradigmatic example of ideal theory is John Rawls's *Theory of Justice* (Cambridge, MA: Belknap Press of Harvard University Press, 1971, 2002). Non-ideal theory, on the other hand, focuses on unjust situations and ways to develop conceptual and analytic tools to diagnose and remedy existing injustices. Some of the main proponents of non-ideal theory are Elizabeth Anderson, Charles Mills, and Amartya Sen.

19. Hillary Clinton talks about this phenomenon in her memoirs: "At the beginning of the campaign, Isabelle and Barbara got me ready for the day once a week or so, as well as for big events such as debates. I tried to take care of my own hair and makeup the rest of the time. But photos don't lie, and since I looked better when they were with me, it became an everyday thing. . . . I've never gotten used to how much effort it takes just to be a woman in the public eye. I once calculated how many hours I spent having my hair and makeup done during the campaign. It came to about six hundred hours, or twenty-five days! . . . I'm not jealous of my male colleagues often, but I am when it comes to how they can just shower, shave, put on a suit, and be ready to go. The few times I've gone out in public without makeup, it's made the news." Hillary Rodham Clinton, *What Happened* (New York: Simon and Schuster, 2017).

20. Ann Cudd, "Oppression by Choice," *Journal of Social Philosophy* 25 (1994): 22–44.

21. For instance, "Most women both claim and detest their feminine condition; they experience it in resentment." Beauvoir, *The Second Sex*, 562.

22. Ibid., 45, translation modified.

23. Ibid., 764.

24. Sonia Kruks, in *Simone de Beauvoir and the Politics of Ambiguity*, demonstrates that Beauvoir's work is crucial to understanding what privilege is. See chapter 3, titled "Confronting Privilege," 93–123.

25. Beauvoir, *The Second Sex*, 759.

26. Ibid., 760.

27. The term "brotherhood," which could also be translated as "fraternity," comes as much more of a surprise to the English reader than to the French one. Beauvoir refers here to "fraternité," which is one of the three concepts of the motto of the French republic ("Liberté, égalité, fraternité") and was a core value of the French Resistance to Nazi Germany. The fact that she would use this word can be surprising as it appears that she endorses masculine values. After all, the French feminist Olympe de Gouges was already highlighting the way in which this concept erases women during the French Revolution, at the end of the eighteenth century. But in *The Second Sex* Beauvoir is more an existentialist than a feminist and uses a vocabulary that reflects this commitment (she also uses "man" to mean "human being," for instance).

28. Beauvoir, *The Second Sex*, 766, translation modified.

29. Ibid., 513.

Conclusion: What Now?

1. Source: https://www.rainn.org/statistics/criminal-justice-system.

2. In 1991, Anita Hill, a lawyer and an academic, accused then U.S Supreme Court nominee Clarence Thomas of sexual harassment and was called to testify during the Senate Judiciary Committee hearings on Thomas's nomination. In 2018, Christine Blasey Ford, a professor of psychology, accused then U.S. Supreme Court nominee Brett Kavanaugh of sexual assault and was called to testify during the Senate Judiciary Committee hearings on Kavanaugh's nomination. Both of their testimonies were deemed insufficient to block the nomination of their attackers, both were publicly shamed and accused of being liars, and both were victims of threats and intimidation in the aftermath of their testimonies. For a detailed analysis of the Kavanaugh hearings, see Kate Manne, *Entitled: How Male Privilege Hurts Women* (New York: Crown, 2020).

3. The precise evaluation of the prevalence of false allegations of sexual assault is a very contentious matter; social scientists estimate that 2 to 10 percent of sexual assault allegations are false. See David Lisak, Lori Gardinier, et al., "False Allegations of Sexual Assault: An Analysis of Ten Years of Reported Cases," *Violence against Women* 16, no. 12 (2010): 1318–34. However, there is a long-standing dispute between criminal justice professionals and researchers on this issue. See Candida Saunders, "The Truth, the Half-Truth, and Nothing Like the Truth: Reconceptualizing False Allegations of Rape," *British Journal of Criminology* 52, no. 6 (2012): 1152–71.

INDEX